INDONESIA

Text by Elizabeth Mortlock

Photographs by Ashley Baker,
Mark Edleson, Jacqueline Chauvin,
Nilu Sood, Saker Mistri, Steve Baker,
Mary Edleson, Iwan Tirta, Elizabeth Mortlock
and the Indonesian Directorate-General of Tourism

GW00493697

MPC

Published by CFW Publications Ltd.
1602 Alliance Building
130 Connaught Road Central
Hong Kong

Published in the UK and Europe by
Moorland Publishing Co Ltd,
Moor Farm Road, Airfield Estate,
Ashbourne, Derbyshire,
DE6 1HD, England

Printed in Hong Kong

Acknowledgements
My grateful thanks go to Ashley Baker, who did the photo research for this book and generously shared with me her travel experiences in Indonesia, as did Patricia Bacon, Annette Berra, Beverly Campbell, Eleanor Early, Linda Garland, Debby Gibbs, Saker Mistri, David Mortlock, Ni Wayan Murni, Sarah Roberts, Jean Scandlyn and Carol Shattuck. Thanks are also due for the reference resources provided by the Ganesha Volunteers, the American Women's Association (Jakarta), the Parents' Association of the Medan International School, Bapak Dalimunthe of the Directorate-General of Tourism of Indonesia, Hardyanto Hasono of Tedjo Express, the Badung (Bali) Tourist Promotion Board and the Bali Regional Tourist Office.

Cover photo: *Balinese dancer*

Other titles available in the POST GUIDE series:

Hong Kong
Japan
Malaysia
Singapore
Sri Lanka
Thailand
The Philippines

ISBN 0-86190-207-6

Contents

Introduction 7
    Population and Language 8
    The Land 9
    Religion 9
    History and Culture 10
General Information
    Climate 18
    When to Go 18
    What to Pack 18
    Immigration 18
    Customs 19
    Arrival and Departure 19
    Transportation 19
    Tours and Cruises 20
    Hotels 22
    Office Hours 23
    Communications 24
    Media 24
    Health 24
    Money 25
    Children 25
    Bathrooms 26
Highlights of Indonesia
    Shopping 26
    Sports and Recreation 28
    Arts and Entertainment 29
    Festivals and Holidays 29
    Flora and Fauna 29
    Photography 30
    Food and Drink 30
    Etiquette 31
    Suggested Reading 32
Destinations
    Jakarta 33
    Sightseeing 37
    Shopping 44
    Sports and Recreation 47
    Cultural Programmes 49
    Nightlife 49
    Hotels 50
    Restaurants 53

West Java 56
Bogor 56
Puncak 57
Bandung 57
Cirebon 60
The Thousand Islands 61
Samudra Beach 62
Carita Beach 63
Central Java 64
Yogyakarta 65
Solo (Surakarta) 73
East Java 77
Surabaya 80
Madura 83
Tretes 84
Mount Bromo 84
Malang and the Temples 85
Bali 87
Hotels 89
Ubud 96
Restaurants 97
Nightlife 100
Sightseeing 100
Shopping 105
Sports 109
Sumatra 111
Medan 114
Lake Toba 116
West Sumatra 121
Padang 122
Bukittinggi 124
Sulawesi 125
Ujung Pandang 126
Tanah Toraja . , ... 129
North Sulawesi (Manado) 132
Indonesian Words and Phrases 133
Index 139

Prices quoted throughout are in US$ or Indonesian rupiah (Rps)

Introduction

Arrive in Indonesia and your mind becomes a sponge, soaking up impressions at once wonderful, confusing, peaceful, stimulating and thought-provoking.

Impressions will seep in without your even being aware—the distinctive and omnipresent smell of clove-scented cigarettes that crackle when the smoker draws on them, the heavy perfumes of frangipani and ginger flowers. Your cloudy contact lenses will clear with tears as you bite into spicy Padang food, and as you finish a tasty plate of barbecued chicken on bamboo skewers you'll make a mental note to try cooking *sate* yourself when you go home.

Ask for directions and you are likely to get every answer in the book: a blank stare, a half-hearted 'Go left' or a confident 'Go right'. Communications can be frustrating. Stay calm and pleasant and you'll be amazed how the situation will somehow resolve itself with smiles exchanged, coffee offered, your impatient children amused and coddled. Someone may appear, friendly and helpful, offering to guide you personally to where you want to go.

If you usually spend your days at home in a concrete office building or in front of a sink full of dirty dishes, you'll savour lounging on the beach in Bali, sipping coconut juice through a straw from a freshly cut coconut. Perhaps you'll feel your heart pound with excitement as you snorkel on the ocean's surface in the Thousand Islands, getting your first glimpse of the fantastic, vibrant colours of tropical fish darting in and out of undulating banks of live coral.

If you are a history buff you'll have an intellectually stimulating time sorting out regional history that goes back to prehistoric man and which, over the centuries, has absorbed religious and cultural influences from Europe, India, China and the Middle East.

Treasure hunters will discover porcelains, opals and antique textiles. Souvenir hunters will stuff their suitcases with batik place-mats, *wayang* puppets and silver filigree jewellery. Teenagers will find a whole new colourful summer wardrobe in the clothing stalls of Bali for little more than the price of a single outfit back home.

When you are on vacation progress will probably be the last thing on your mind, but progress will be all around you, cutting a path for the future of the country. Children in crisp, clean white blouses walk down village lanes to public schools; government officials attend classes on ideology and compile extensive studies on town planning. City huts give way to modern office towers. Family planning officials gather women dressed in traditional sarongs to learn about Keluarga Berencana, the highly successful family planning programme. Documentaries on television show the transfer of technology by big foreign oil companies to local technicians and engineers.

You'll catch a glimpse of progress, but what will draw you closer to Indonesia, and what will stay in your memory long after you return home, will be the impressions that are timeless: the endearing smile of a child perched on the back of his family's water buffalo; a volcano hazy on the horizon; rice terraces emerald green in the afternoon sun; roadside stalls dimly lit by gas lanterns; comely dancers in glittering costumes flashing their eyes to the music of a *gamelan* orchestra.

Back in your hotel your head will be full of impressions. If you are in five-star, big-city luxury, there will be an orchid at your bedside, a breakfast order card to hang on your door handle. If you are in a Balinese cottage you'll gaze up at the marvellous thatched roof, feel the cool breeze from the ceiling fan whirring above, listen to the '*cicak*' of the little lizard over the door frame.

Give your five senses a break and have a good sleep, for tomorrow there will be a fresh onslaught of impressions of a richly interesting country— Indonesia.

Population and Language

With 150 million people, Indonesia is the fifth most populous country in the world after China, India, the Soviet Union and the United States. The population is unevenly distributed, and 65 percent (some 90 million people) is packed into the relatively small island of Java. To rectify this problem the government has started a transmigration programme aimed at relocating Javanese to other, less populous islands. More than half of the people are under 20 years of age, and 83 percent are rural peasants. They are mainly of Malay heritage: Proto- and Deutero-Malay with mixtures of Melanesoid and Negrito races.

The national motto is *Bhinneka Tunggal Ika,* which means 'Unity in Diversity'. Great diversity is found in Indonesia's 366 ethnic groups, some with vastly differing local languages and customs, known as *adat*. Indonesians are generally proud of their individual ethnic origins, yet are tolerant of other people's ways and beliefs, whether Indonesian or foreign.

The national language, Bahasa Indonesia, unites a nation where regional languages and dialects are still spoken. Bahasa (which literally means 'language') is much like Malay and uses Roman script and alphabet. See the section on *Words and Phrases* (page 133) and give it a try. It's not difficult to pronounce and the grammar is uncomplicated. Your most feeble attempts will be greeted with a smiling approval.

The educated older generation can often speak Dutch, a hold-over from colonial days. English is spoken by some, particularly in the major business and tourist areas.

The Land

Indonesia is the world's largest archipelago, comprising 13,600 islands of which 6,100 are inhabited. Lying along the equator between the Asian mainland and Australia, Indonesia spans 3,200 miles (5,120 kms), roughly the same as the United States.
The largest islands are Sumatra, Java, Kalimantan (formerly Borneo, now shared with Malaysia), Sulawesi and Irian Jaya (the western part of New Guinea). Chains of mountains and volcanoes give shape to the islands of Sumatra, Java and Bali. Of 300 volcanoes, 128 are active. Lava and volcanic ash add to the fertility of the soil and create a lush tropical vegetation. But fear not, volcanic eruptions should pose no threat to your holiday.

Religion

Although Indonesia is predominantly Muslim, it is not fanatically so, and there is a harmonious coexistence among religions. Some 87 percent of the population is Muslim, seven percent Christian, three percent Hindu or Buddhist, with the rest following indigenous animism and other beliefs. Christianity is the main religion in North Sulawesi, the Moluccas, Flores, Timor and Irian Jaya as well as among the Batak of North Sumatra. Bali is predominantly Hindu.
Observing religious customs may be an interesting part of your stay in Indonesia. Every Friday you will see men and boys dressed in plaid sarongs and black caps (known as *pici*) swarm to the mosque (*mesjid*) for prayers. A white cap indicates a *haji*, one who has made the pilgrimage to Mecca. You may awaken in the pre-dawn stillness to the day's first call to prayer. Some Muslims devoutly pray five times a day at home, at the office or in small village prayer halls known as *musholla*. Others are less devout, praying less often perhaps, but always celebrating Lebaran, the Muslim holiday which follows the month of daytime fasting.
When visiting a mosque, dress conservatively (no shorts or revealing clothing) and remove your shoes before entering. If a caretaker is around, ask his permission (usually freely given) to enter. When visiting a Christian church service, feel free to join the congregation in well-known Christian hymns which may be sung in English, Batak, Chinese or Indonesian.
The Hindu religion of Bali is cause for almost constant colourful ceremonial celebration and prayer in regional, village and family temples. The Balinese are used to tourists attending their ceremonies, though visitors should remember the essential religious nature of these ceremonies and be respectful, especially when observing quiet prayers inside temples. As one Balinese said, with her ever gracious smile, 'Some visitors seem to forget that Bali is *not* Disneyland. Everything here is not done just to amuse the tourists.' In Bali menstruating women should honour local custom by not entering temples, and a sash (available all over Bali for one or two US

Muslim schoolgirls in North Sumatra

dollars) should be worn by men and women alike when visiting a temple.

Buddhism is practised in Chinese temples *(klenteng)*, which you can find in Jakarta, Semarang, Solo and elsewhere. Supplicants light joss sticks for good luck and prosperity, and fortunes are read in Chinese or Bahasa Indonesia. Every year Buddhists gather to celebrate Waisak, the Buddhist holiday, at the Borobudur monument and at the nearby Candi Mendut.

While each of these major religions has taken hold in Indonesia, they are often overlaid with animism and ancestor worship, the oldest spiritual beliefs of Indonesia's earliest peoples. A person may devoutly follow Islam, Christianity or Hinduism and at the same time maintain a special awareness of the mystical forces that surround him.

History and Culture

Diverse cultural influences have strongly affected some parts of Indonesia, while other parts remain remote and isolated. The result is a complex mosaic of history, traditions, arts and culture.

There's no better place to begin to grasp the long history and cultural diversity of Indonesia than at the National Museum in Jakarta. Casts of Java Man's skull and femur are on display. The originals were discovered in Central Java in 1891, proving that man lived in the archipelago as early as 500,000 years ago. Simple stone tools and axe handles of semi-precious stone are also testimony to the existence of man in the New Stone Age about 4,000 years ago. Bronze Age finds in Indonesia date back to 300 BC, and include bronze thunder drums decorated with symbols and motifs of an animistic religion. These drums are typical of the Southeast Asian Dong Son culture that extended from China through Vietnam, Laos, Cambodia, Thailand and on to Indonesia.

Where did Indonesia's earliest inhabitants come from? The museum's enormous map shows that in prehistoric times Indonesia was connected by a giant land bridge from the Asian mainland down the Malay Peninsula to Sumatra, Java and Bali. Asian people migrated along this bridge. A land bridge also connected the eastern islands of Indonesia with New Guinea and Australia. A northern land bridge joined the Philippines to Sulawesi. The islands of Indonesia were created when, at the end of the Ice Age, the ice of the northern hemisphere melted, raising the water level and creating a sea that separated the newly-formed islands of the archipelago.

Indonesia's earliest people were hunters and gatherers, living on shellfish, wild fruits, roots, seeds and the meat of wild elephant, deer, pig and rhinoceros that roamed the land. No doubt they were animistic in their beliefs. Living so closely with nature's creative and destructive forces, it is not surprising that they identified spirits to be worshipped and placated.

Buddhists celebrate Waisak at the Borobudur Temple

To imagine the life of these early people, look around the museum's ethnography section, particularly the Irian Jaya displays, where you will see that some of the isolated tribes of Indonesia retained their Stone Age, primitive lifestyle right up to the 20th century. Using digging sticks for agriculture, wearing only gourds and decorating their hair with bird feathers, the men of the Baliem Valley were only recently discovered by outsiders. Ritual warfare and head-hunting played an important part in their society until it was banned earlier in this century.

For centuries the people of Indonesia have lived in rural outdoor settings and created the necessities of life from materials close at hand, just as most of them still do today. In the National Museum you'll see *ikat* cloth, for example, homespun on the island of Sumba and dyed with natural dyes from available roots and plants. The ethnography section is packed with items created just as they have been for centuries in rural Indonesia— baskets of palm fibres, a mandolin made from a palm leaf, shields painted with natural dyes.

Other parts of Indonesia, however, were less isolated and came into

contact with external forces from other countries of Asia. Traders from India and China came to the coastal ports and brought with them fabulous silks with golden threads such as those still worn at traditional weddings in South Sumatra.

Also from India came Hinduism and Buddhism. From AD 760 to 1520, Indonesian Hindu and Buddhist kingdoms (among them Srivijaya and Majapahit) played powerful roles in Sumatra, Java and the region. In the National Museum in Jakarta you will see stone sculptures of the Hindu gods Brahma, Vishnu and Shiva and enormous, calm, meditating stone Buddhas. Hinduism and Buddhism coexisted congenially in Indonesia.

The local rulers of the Javanese kingdoms welcomed Indian beliefs, especially the belief in the divine nature of kings, and in Central and East Java you will see small temples, known as *candi*, which were temples to the Hindu and Buddhist deities and their earthly incarnations, the local rulers. Also in the area of Yogyakarta be sure to visit the splendid Borobudur, built in about AD 800 and one of the world's most impressive Buddhist monuments, as well as the Prambanan temple complex, a fine example of

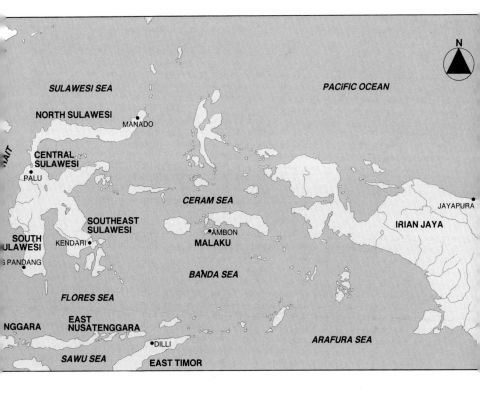

Dani tribesmen of the Baliem Valley, Irian Jaya

Hindu religious architecture of the same period. But Hinduism and Buddhism were to lose their hold on Java. The Arabs first landed in North Sumatra in AD 846 and Muslim kingdoms arose in Java in the 16th century with the spread of Islam throughout the islands. As Islam took over in Java, Hinduism moved to Bali where it has stayed, playing a key role in the daily lives of the people. At Bali's famous Besakih Temple, which flanks a mountainside and commands a splendid view, there are pavilions erected to house the three Hindu gods Brahma, Vishnu and Shiva. Also following Hindu tradition, Balinese identify each other by caste names, and bodies are cremated at death—a cause for celebration, as the spirit is freed to take its place in the cosmic order of things.

In Java, Muslim sultans maintained their courts, or *kraton*, which tourists enjoy visiting in Yogyakarta and Surakarta (Solo) in Central Java. This *kraton* culture is the source of so much that is recognised as typically Javanese art and culture today. Royal entertainment was, and is, provided by the *gamelan* orchestra accompanying a slow, refined dance. When you attend a performance, listen for the sound of the individual instruments: the metallaphones, the gongs big and booming or short and squat, the *rebab* (a violin that sounds persistently off-key to the Western ear) and the *gambang*, a type of xylophone. As your ear becomes accustomed to the music, you'll begin to notice punctuations created by the gongs to mark the

Women making batik cloth

sections of the piece, and the changes in rhythm signalled by the drummer.

Princesses, kept safe within the *kraton* walls, passed the hours creating batik. The process is slow, requiring a steady hand and hours of careful application of liquid wax on to the material. The wax provides a protective coating, so that when the material is dyed the design created in wax remains white. Subsequent waxing and dyeing create additional patterns and colours. It was said that a woman's character and strength of self-discipline could be judged by the quality of her batik.

Today's Javanese princesses are too busy with university studies, and the palace craft is done in factories and small home industries. When you visit these workshops in Jakarta and Central Java you can see women making batik in the traditional way, using the *canting*, or wax-filled pen. Men at one side of the workshop sidestep this tedious process by applying the wax with a copper stamp of the design, completing the job in record time.

While Muslim sultans ruled their people from the palaces of Java, still another cultural wave was pounding at Indonesia's shores. European traders came to Indonesia's islands, which were rich in spices, a bounty for those who dealt in them. Pepper, cloves and nutmeg all had high value in the international market.

The Portuguese arrived in the Spice Islands (Maluku) in the 16th century, followed closely by the Dutch. In 1621 the Dutch defeated the local rulers and set up their headquarters in the old part of modern-day Jakarta. Naming their walled city Batavia, these traders of the Dutch East India Company (VOC) braved cholera, malaria and the long ocean voyage in the hopes of financial success in the spice trade.

Their power spread in the archipelago, and they built enclaves of Dutch life to maintain their hold on the islands: Fort Speelwijk in Banten, West Java; mountain retreat homes for Dutch rubber planters in Brastagi, North Sumatra; administrative buildings within the fort in Ujung Pandang, South Sulawesi. Today Indonesia's main cities and towns almost always have Dutch-built office buildings and areas of handsome villas to remind us of colonial days.

The Dutch, who had initially come only for profit, developed their colonial power, and many intermarried and stayed for generations. Indonesia became their home. They built the railway system that you can take from Jakarta to the mountain city of Bandung, and they collected most of the treasures housed in the National Museum.

Dutch suzerainty in Indonesia lasted for nearly 350 years, interrupted only briefly from 1811 to 1816 when Indonesia fell under British East India Company rule. The British were led by Sir Stamford Raffles, who wrote the enormously detailed *History of Java*, a classic even today, and who later went on to found Singapore. Dutch rule was also challenged during scattered wars with local people, but it was not until the 1940s that their colonial domination was finally eclipsed.

The door to independence was opened in 1942 when Indonesia was invaded by the Japanese, who unseated the Dutch as masters. When the Japanese occupation ended in 1945, the Indonesian nationalists, led by the charismatic Sukarno, called for *merdeka*, or freedom. Reluctant to give up their colonial treasure, the Dutch fought to regain power. But they were unsuccessful, and in 1949 the Republic of Indonesia was officially recognised as an independent country under President Sukarno. The red and white flag of the new nation was raised, people cheered and then set to work to face the challenges of building a new nation.

Sukarno sought to make Jakarta a jewel in the crown of Indonesia. In the run-down city, where services were lacking and life was hard for the ordinary man, he built impressive structures with Russian assistance—the Senayan Sports Stadium, vigorous patriotic monuments at the new traffic circles, and Sarinah's Department Store, named after his childhood maid.

But Sukarno's power, once so strong, was to falter. On the night of September 30, 1965, participants in a communist-inspired coup slaughtered six leading generals. Anti-communist reaction was immediate. Soon afterwards Sukarno, in poor health, stepped down to be replaced by Suharto, the next light on the new nation's horizon.

Modern national development has leapt ahead under President Suharto, recently elected to his fourth term as the second president of Indonesia. It is under the leadership of this popular statesman, almost always seen in public with his wife Ibu Tien, that Indonesia has developed. The president is elected to five-year terms by the People's Consultative Assembly, the highest government body, to which members are elected and appointed. There are three main political parties: Golkar, the Muslim United Development Party and the Indonesian Democratic Party. As head of government, the president is assisted by a cabinet of ministers who serve as advisers, but who have no legislative power.

The principles of Pancasila, the state philosophy originally created by President Sukarno, have been constantly restated, and all government officials have undergone study to ensure that their understanding of the five principles is complete. The principles are: belief in one supreme god, belief in a just and civilised humanity, belief in Indonesian unity, belief in the sovereignty of the people guided by the wisdom of unanimity in deliberations among representatives, and belief in social justice for all people.

The economy of Indonesia today relies on its natural resources. Rich volcanic soils have allowed for the widespread development of agriculture on the islands of Sumatra, Java and Bali. The main crops are rice, corn, cassava, coconut, soyabean, sugar, palm oil, coffee, tea, tobacco and spices.

Indonesia is also a major source of petroleum, natural gas, timber, tin, bauxite, nickel, copper and coal. However, much of the country has yet to be surveyed geologically. Smallholder agriculture employs about 60 percent of the labour force, consisting mainly of food crops for domestic consumption and export.

Tin has historically been the country's primary mineral export, although the importance of oil has increased greatly in recent years and it is now the biggest earner of foreign exchange. In 1981, under the state oil company Pertamina, oil and gas contributed about 70 percent of Indonesian government revenues and foreign exchange earnings. With the recent reduction in the price of oil, emphasis on tourism and non-oil exports has increased.

In the manufacturing sector, production of many commodities like textiles, pharmaceuticals, fertiliser, cement, automobiles and electronic goods for the domestic market has expanded rapidly and become of increasing importance to the economy.

Foreign investment, rejected during the Sukarno period, has been welcomed back into the country, with the proviso that foreign workers transfer their technical knowledge to Indonesian workers. Major investment has come from Japan, Hong Kong, the United States, Canada, the Netherlands and West Germany, and many projects have been developed in the fields of agriculture, forestry, fishing, mining, manufacturing, construction, trading, hotels, real estate, transportation and services.

General Information

Climate

Only two seasons: dry (May-October) and wet (November-April) with average rainfall 40 inches. Temperature in coastal areas is 23-33° Celsius, with evenings cooled by breezes. Inner lowlands are 20-30°C (68-86° Fahrenheit). Highlands are 16-26°C, with freezing temperatures only on high mountain slopes exceeding 10,000 feet. Average humidity 69-95 percent. From a practical point of view, this means it is very hot by day, not as hot in the evening and cool during the evening in the mountains.

When to Go

Any time is a good time to visit, as even in the rainy season thunderstorms are interspersed with bright sunshine. However, during the rainy season travel may be hampered by flooding.

What to Pack

Dress is normally casual in Indonesia, and light clothing is advisable due to the hot, humid climate. Jacket and tie are required only for formal occasions or when making official calls. For normal business calls, a shirt and tie or leisure suit are appropriate. Formal evening wear is the widely available long-sleeved batik shirt worn with dark trousers. For travel in mountain areas a sweater or light jacket may be necessary.

Women should dress modestly, avoiding scanty blouses and shorts. Skimpy beachwear is only appropriate at the beach in tourist areas. For sightseeing make sure to have shoes that can get wet or muddy without causing you great distress.

It's handy to bring along sunglasses, film, mosquito repellent, flashlight, a roll of toilet paper, a plastic water container for sightseeing trips, and suntan lotion. Electrical current in most hotels is 220 volts, 50 cycles with a two-pronged plug, although some hotels still have 110 volts, so check with your hotel before plugging in your hairdryer. Bring along any prescription drugs you normally take, an antiseptic to clean cuts, as well as medicine in case you run into a bout of upset stomach or diarrhoea.

Immigration

All travellers to Indonesia must be in possession of a passport valid for at least six months, with proof of onward passage. As of August 1987 visas were waived for nationals of 30 countries for tourist visits of no more than two months. These countries are: Australia, Austria, Belgium, Brunei, Canada, Denmark, Finland, France, Great Britain, Greece, Iceland, Ireland, Italy, Japan, Liechtenstein, Luxemburg, Malaysia, Malta, the Netherlands, New

Zealand, Norway, the Philippines, Singapore, South Korea, Spain, Sweden, Switzerland, Thailand, the United States and West Germany.

Visa-free entry is available through the airports of Jakarta, Bali, Medan, Batam, Pekanbaru, Padang, Manado, Ambon, Biak, Kupung and Pontianak, and the seaports of Jakarta, Surabaya, Bali (Benoa and Padang Bai) Medan, Ambon, Manado (Bitung) and semarang (Tanjung Mas).

The two-month tourist visa is not extendible.

For nationals of other countries not specified above, tourist visas can be obtained from any Indonesian embassy or consulate on payment of visa fees. Two photographs are required.

Customs

Customs allows on entry a maximum of two litres of alcoholic beverages, 200 cigarettes or 50 cigars or 100 grams of tobacco and a reasonable amount of perfume per adult. Cars, photographic equipment, typewriters and radios are admitted provided they are taken out on departure. They must be declared to Customs. There is no restriction on import or export of foreign currencies and traveller's cheques, but the import or export of Indonesian currency exceeding Rps 50,000 is prohibited.

Arrival and Departure

International flights arrive in Jakarta at Halim Perdanakusuma Airport. Domestic flights from Jakarta to Denpasar (Bali) and Yogyakarta also leave from Halim. Other domestic flights from Jakarta leave from Kemayoran Airport. A new Jakarta international and domestic airport at Cengkareng is under construction, and scheduled for completion in mid-1985.

There is an airport departure tax of Rps 9,000 per person for flights on international routes from Jakarta, Medan, Manado, Biak, Denpasar and Ambon. Airport tax on domestic routes is Rps 1,200 to 2,000.

For international departures, permanent residents of Indonesia must pay a fiscal tax of Rps 150,000 per person. Foreign residents of Indonesia must have a valid exit/re-entry permit in order to leave and re-enter Indonesia.

Transportation

City to City: By far the easiest and most pleasant means of travel is by air on the domestic routes of Garuda, Merpati, Mandala or Bouraq airlines. Within Java one can travel by train on the overnight *Bima* train from Jakarta to Surabaya via Yogyakarta. One-way tickets are available from Carnation Travel, Jl. Menteng Raya, Jakarta.

Public bus travel is available but not recommended as it may be overcrowded and uncomfortable. Hiring a car and driver at your hotel is the best way to travel short distances between cities that have no air connection. Because prices for a car and driver are reasonable (about

US$40 to $90 per day) and driving can be very harried, most tourists do not drive themselves.

Within a City: Jakarta has taxis which can be flagged down on the street or summoned by telephone (Blue Bird Taxi: Tel. 325607, 334397).

In other places the most common way for visitors to travel within a city is by tour bus or by hiring a car and driver at your hotel (about US$3.50-$5 per hour). Fees can be by the trip, by the hour or by the day. Ask your hotel for suggested fares. Bargaining may be necessary.

In smaller cities or towns you may enjoy riding short distances in colourful local transportation. A *bemo* (or colt) is a small, open-backed mini-truck that plies a given route. You can flag them down on the road. Signal the driver when you want to get off and pay the established fare (cheap). There are always surprises on *bemos*. You may share your seat with a basket of live chickens or a palm tree trunk on its way to a traditional puppet performance. (If you're wondering why anyone would need a tree trunk at a puppet show, the answer is that the puppets are displayed by sticking their handles firmly into the tree trunk, which lies horizontally under the screen.) Sometimes a *bemo* with driver can be chartered by the hour or by the day for your personal use.

Becaks are also very popular. You sit in a covered seat and the driver, perched on a bicycle seat behind you, will pedal you to where you want to go. Just flag down a free driver, bargain on a price by the hour or according to the destination, and pay at the end of the ride. Can be unnerving as you swoop in and out of traffic. Safer on quiet side streets.

Delman or *dokar* are old-fashioned horse and buggies. Tell your driver you want a one or two-hour city tour, returning to your starting point. Bargain on the price before getting in, then watch the sights slip by to the clip-clop of the horse's feet. Call out '*Tolong berhenti*' ('Please stop') when you want to investigate something.

Taxi drivers usually speak only very limited English, if any. With *bemo*, *becak* and *delman* drivers you'll have to rely on sign language, goodwill and perhaps some assistance from your hotel.

Tours and Cruises

While independent travellers will enjoy Jakarta, Yogyakarta and Bali on their own, other destinations require greater flexibility on the part of the traveller, because little English may be spoken and transportation may not be readily available. A tour will take the wear and tear out of planning, sightseeing, hotels and transportation.

Garuda Indonesian Airways offers holiday packages for the independent traveller in Indonesia. Each package includes accommodation, sightseeing, transfers and breakfast. Prices are per person for twin sharing. Airline transportation to the destination is extra. Two-night, three-day packages are available in Jakarta (US$39-$159), Pulau Putri ($136), Samudra Beach ($150), Yogyakarta ($44-$85), Solo ($82-$98), Semarang ($100-$120), Surabaya ($60-$130), Flores ($144), Bali Handara Country Club ($95), Ambon ($184), Lombox ($80-$100) and Bandung ($49-$83).

Three-night, four-day packages are: Bali ($66-$156; a *really* good deal), Manado ($182-$206), Toraja ($215-$240) and Mahakam River, Kalimantan ($417). A four-night, five-day is available to Lake Toba ($116). For further information contact the nearest Garuda office or Satriaui Tours and Travel, Jl. Prapatan 32, P.O. Box 2536, Jakarta, Tel. 353543, Telex 45745 RYATUR 1A.

Package tours are also arranged by Pacto Ltd, Hotel Borobudur, Jl. Lapangan Banteng, Jakarta, Tel. 370108, 356952, Telex JKT 47582. For the real adventurer, very unusual tours (such as trekking into the primitive Baliem Valley of Irian Jaya or going by riverboat to tribal villages in Kalimantan) are capably led by Ms Sjam of Tambora Tour Division. Jl. Prapanca Raya 24, Kebayoran Baru, Jakarta Selatan, Tel. 717849, Telex 45755 MANDA JKT.

Bus Tours: Java-Bali overland bus tours are offered by Garuda and are available for $389-$454 per person including hotel, meals, service charges and taxes. A sumatra overland tour for $328 is also offered.

The well-known travel agencies Pacto, Nitour, Tunas and Vayatour have representative offices in most cities, where you can arrange one to three-day local bus tours.

Cruise Ships: Many luxury liners call at Indonesian ports. Some, like the *Royal Viking Star*, only come to Indonesia once or twice a year. Others, such as the *Coral Princess*, the *Golden Odyssey*, the *Princess Mahsuri* and the *Pearl of Scandinavia*, come as often as once a month during certain months of the year. Of course, schedules and price are subject to change without notice.

The *Princess Mahsuri* is a German-built and owned ship with 150 first-class cabins. Its 14-day cruise (Singapore, Penang, Phuket, Nias, Padang, Jakarta, Bali, Surabaya, Singapore) is US$2,240-$4,460 per person. If you don't have the time (or the money!), try the five-day Jakarta, Bali, Surabaya tour ($680-$1,200 per person including Surabaya—Jakarta airfare). For information contact Blue Funnel Cruises (10 Collyer Quay, #06-07 Ocean Building, Singapore 0104, Tel. 5336071, Telex RS 28550 BF CRU) or contact Setia Tours (Jl. Pinangsia Raya, Glodok Plaza, Blok B, No. 1, Jakarta, Tel. 630008, P.O. Box 1104 Jakarta Kota, Telex 41290).

The *Pearl of Scandinavia* makes 14-day cruises from Singapore to Medan, Penang, Sibolga, Nias, Jakarta, Bali, Surabaya, Jakarta and back to Singapore for US$1,960-$6,230 per person. The five-day Jakarta—Jakarta segment is $700-$2,225. Reservations through your local travel agent or Nitour, Jl. Majapahit 2, Jakarta, Tel. 346349.

Candi Kidal, a typical East Java temple

Travel by Boat: Though not a cruise ship with tourist facilities, the SS *Kerinci* is a new Indonesian ship with decent accommodations which sails from Jakarta to Padang, West Sumatra, every Friday at 1pm and from Padang to Jakarta Sunday at 11pm.

The trip takes 30 hours. First-class cabins accommodate two poeple each and second class berths four. There is a Bar and Dining room.

The *Kerinci* sails from Jakarta to Ujung Pandang, South Sulawesi, every Tuesday evening at 5pm and departs Ujung Pandang for Jaklarta every Wednesday at 10am. It is a 40-hour trip with first-class and second-class on board. Tickets available through Tambora Pariwisata Indah, Jl. Sultan Hasanuddin, Kebayoran Baru, Jakarta, Tel. 776193.

Hotels

Hotels in Indonesia range from de luxe, five-star establishments with glamorous lobbies and every facility, to little guest houses where you may shower the traditional way by splashing yourself with cold water from a tub.

Five-star hotels are the equal of their counterparts anywhere in the world. Four-star hotels also usually offer all the facilities of a big hotel.

Pig feast in the Baliem Valley, Irian Jaya

Three and two-star hotels usually have airconditioned rooms, attached bathrooms, hot and cold running water, telephones and restaurants. A three-star hotel may have a swimming pool. One-star hotels may have airconditioned rooms and attached bath. Prices fluctuate from hotel to hotel, place to place, season to season. Roughly speaking, prices for a double in Jakarta are: four and five-star hotel (US$50-$175), three-star ($40-$100), two-star ($10-45). All rates include tax and service. Outside the capital, of course, rates can be more attractive.

In Bali especially, one can find pleasant homestays for only a few dollars per night where you will have your own room in the family house or compound. Just look for the signs saying 'Homestay' in the Peliaten-Ubud area of Bali.

Hotels in this guide are listed under specific location. This will allow you to choose a nice hotel which fits in well with your tour itinerary.

Office Hours

Offices are open from 8.30am until 4.30 or 5pm. Most are open on Saturdays from 8.30am to 12.30pm. Government offices and government museums are usually open for 8am until 2pm, except on Fridays (8-11.30am) and Saturdays (8am-2pm). Museums are often open on Sunday mornings, but may be closed on Mondays.

Communications

Mail, cable, telex, local and international telephone facilities are available in all big cities and major tourist areas. Most big hotels have telephones for local and international calls in the rooms. It is generally faster and safer to hand-carry your purchases than to mail them. Mail service is less than reliable.

Media

Three English-language daily newspapers are published in Jakarta: the *Jakarta Post*, the *Indonesian Observer* and the *Indonesian Times*. They are available at the newsstands of big hotels. The *Asian Wall Street Journal* and the *International Herald Tribune* are also available at most five-star hotels.

Television and radio are controlled by the government-owned Radio Republic Indonesia. In Jakarta children's TV programmes in English are broadcast at 5.30pm, and there is an English-language newscast at 6.30pm. Many hotels have in-house video programmes in English.

Health

International certificates of valid smallpox, cholera and yellow fever vaccinations are required only for travellers coming from infected areas. Typhoid and paratyphoid vaccinations are not required but are advisable. Cholera may also be advisable but it is of limited protection. Outside urban Jakarta and Surabaya malaria prophylactic tablets (such as Chloroquin and Fansidar) are advisable, to be taken weekly one week before departure until six weeks after returning home.

People who are in poor health should avoid travel to remote areas of Indonesia, as medical facilities are limited, especially in smaller towns and villages. Bring along any medicine you normally take as well as remedies for an upset stomach or diarrhoea. Antiseptic to clean cuts and scrapes may also come in handy.

Never drink or brush your teeth with unboiled water. Most hotels provide boiled water or bottled Aqua water in the room. When in doubt about the water, quench your thirst with beer, name-brand soft drinks, hot tea or coffee. Take along a flask of water when touring for the day. Make sure to drink lots of fluids to avoid dehydration in the tropical sun.

Avoid uncooked food, unpeeled fruits, ice, raw vegetables, milk and ice cream. Hot, freshly prepared food in Chinese and hotel restaurants is usually reliable.

If you need medical attention, consult your hotel information desk and ask them to recommend a reliable doctor and to make an appointment for you. If you have a very serious problem or are hospitalised, it is advisable to have an Indonesian-speaking person accompany you to act as a translator.

Money

Banks are open from 8am until 12 noon or 1pm. some are open from 8-11am on Saturdays. Big hotels have licensed money changers. Traveller's cheques can usually be cashed at your hotel cashier, banks and money changers.

American Express, Diner's Club, Carte Blanche and Bank Americard are generally accepted by the largest hotels. Personal cheques are not accepted.

When buying souvenirs, paying for meals in restaurants, paying taxi drivers and the like it is easiest to use cash. Small shop-owners and taxi drivers may not have change, so be sure to have small denominations on hand. Lots of 1,000-rupiah notes are best to cover small purchases.

As of mid-1987 the exchange rate was Rps 1,600 to US$1. This makes for easy calculations:

Tipping: In most hotels a 21 percent service and government tax is automatically added to your bill. At restaurants where no service charge has been added, a tip of 10 percent is normal. Airport porters expect Rps 500 per bag. Tip a taxi driver Rps 200-300. If you have a driver take you sightseeing for a whole day, a tip of Rps 200 per hour of service is welcome.

Children

Travelling in Indonesia with children is not only possible, but can be a real pleasure for both parents and children. Bali is most popular with families because there is something for everyone—beaches, pools, colourful and entertaining traditional dances as well as stores and doctors to handle emergencies. Jakarta is second best. Here again you'll find nice hotels and good back-up services. Travel to other parts of Indonesia depends on a family's flexibility—heat, lack of baby-sitters, transportation delays and the non-availability of disposable diapers (nappies) and English-speaking doctors can be very bothersome.

Bring along all the disposable diapers and baby formula you will need for your trip, although these are usually in good supply at Galael's supermarket chain in Jakarta and Kuta Beach, Bali.

Where Western food is not available, picky eaters usually enjoy bananas, white rice and chicken *sate* (skewers of barbecued chicken), which are available everywhere. Hamburgers and colas are widely available in major tourist areas.

In the warm tropical environment make sure your children drink lots of fluids. They can drink bottled Aqua water or bottled cola (without ice). When touring look for little boxes of a sweet fruit drink called Buavita, or offer them safe-to-drink Susu Ultra, a long-life milk in a blue box (plain) or tan box (chocolate).

Hand-drawn batik on cotton designed by Iwan Tirta

Bathrooms

Most tourist hotels have Western-style facilities. When sightseeing you will find Asian-style public toilets—hole-in-the-ground style porcelain fixtures. Flush by sluicing the hole with water from the dipper floating in the tub of water in the room, or fill the dipper from the tap. Bring your own toilet tissue.

If you are in a very simple guest house you'll be able to try a *mandi*—a traditional bath. Wear rubber flip-flops into the room. Using the plastic dipper that floats in the tub of water, pour water over yourself on to the floor. *Do not* get into the tub. If you ever get dizzy with heatstroke, simply get out of the sun, ask someone if you can use their *mandi* and splash the cool water over your head. Relax for a while with a Coke or tea.

Highlights of Indonesia

Shopping

The places to shop in Indonesia include shopping centres with fixed prices and a range of luxury items, *tokos* (little stores) *warungs* (roadside stalls) and *pasars* (Asian bazaars that are extremely colourful and informal, packed with fruits and vegetables, handicrafts and baskets, all at low prices).

Bargaining is the rule in Indonesia, a must nearly everywhere except in big, fancy department stores where signs usually proclaim 'harga pas' (fixed price). Just remember that bargaining is not a confrontation. It's a friendly way to settle on a mutually agreeable price. First ask the price, then smile and offer less. The salesman will then counter with a price between his initial price and your offer. In the end you should pay 10-50 percent off the first price named.

During your bargaining ask, 'Can you cut the price a bit?' or 'Can you give me a discount?' You might gently indicate reasons why you probably shouldn't buy the article: 'I don't think my wife will like it' or 'My luggage is full already'. Don't get rude or excited.

Handicrafts in Indonesia are good quality, imaginative and reasonably priced. The best place to get an overall view of what's available from the far-flung corners of Indonesia is at Sarinah's Department Store on Jalan Thamrin in Jakarta. Among the bric-a-brac and real treasures you will find here and in the shops in the places you visit are the following:

Silver—Balinese and Central Javanese silversmiths create demitasse spoons, filigree pins, miniature *becaks*, necklaces and even construction workers' hats richly decorated with oil rigs and tropical plants.

Woodcarving—In Bali woodcarvers abound, making dance masks, serene and fanciful sculptures, napkin rings and cigarette boxes. Indonesia's

Silversmith using a 'blow torch' in Kota Gede, Central Java

talented woodcrafters also create carved wooden chests, baroque bed frames and polychromed Balinese doors that are beautiful to look at but impossible to fit into your airline luggage allowance.

Batik—It seems that no one leaves Indonesia without something in batik—shirts, dresses, toys, tablecloths, place mats and napkins. Batik comes in several qualities, depending on the technique used in its making. Cheapest is fake batik, actually machine-printed material using batik designs. You can tell this material because it is sold in large bolts and has a non-handcrafted, perfect look in the colour and printing. The reverse side of the material does not have the pattern.

Real batik (*cap* or *tulis*) is created by applying a wax design to plain cloth, then dipping the cloth into a dye, leaving the waxed area plain. Successive waxing and dyeing create more complicated patterns and colours. *Cap* batik uses a metal stamp, or *cap*, to stamp the pattern on, quickly repeating the motif over the whole cloth. *Tulis* requires that every line be drawn by hand with a little copper pen filled with liquid wax. Needless to say, because it is so time-consuming, *tulis* batik is the most expensive cloth, running $20-$100 for two metres.

Other Textiles—Batik is only a small part of Indonesia's huge textile heritage. Go to regional *pasars* or markets and buy the plaid sarongs worn to the mosques, *songket* (decorated with supplementary weaving of metallic thread) and *ikat* (identified by the fuzzy outlines on the geometric designs). In Bali you can buy gold-painted textiles (*kain prada*).

Leather Goods—Sandals, camera bags, wallets and purses are available in stiff, tanned leather and reptile skins.

Ceramics—Antique and newly-made ceramics are both available. Buyer beware! The salesman may claim it's Ming, but it may be a skilfully produced copy from Bandung.

Baskets—Baskets in all shapes and sizes make light souvenirs of your holiday. Best selections are usually in the open markets. These are inexpensive and widely used in Indonesian daily life.

Wayang Puppets—The exotic characters of the puppet theatre are available, either as *wayang golek* (wooden-headed dolls on sticks) or *wayang kulit* (puppets carved out of buffalo hide and painted).

Other Surprises—There are lots of things you never knew you needed until you saw them in Indonesia: sachets of herbal medicine (under Air Mancur or Jamu Jago brand names) to cure your flagging sex life, brilliant red-and-gold Balinese umbrellas, Batak calendars carved on a length of bamboo inscribed with illegible characters, and hanging Dutch lamps.

Sports and Recreation

Swimming, diving, golf, hiking, walking, sailing, snorkelling and horseback riding are all available. Check specific sections under each region for details.

Arts and Entertainment

Indonesia's rich cultural heritage and love of music and dance make it an interesting place to take in performances of traditional dance, puppetry and music. Cultural shows are usually available in the big hotels, and you can ask your hotel information desk to recommend local performances of interest. For tour groups special performances of regional dance and music can be arranged on request.

Nightlife for travellers is usually confined to going out to dinner or visiting one of the bars or discotheques in the hotels. Since Indonesia is largely agricultural, the villages close up early, with people going to bed not long after their evening meal and getting up at the crack of dawn.

Festivals and Holidays

Indonesian holidays occur every year on January 1 (New Year's Day), August 17 (Independence Day) and December 25 (Christmas Day).

The date fluctuates for Muslim holidays on the Arabic calendar. Idul Fitri, or Lebaran, falls on the first day of the tenth month of the Arabic calendar. It is preceded by the month of Puasa (Ramadan) when devout Muslims abstain from food and drink during daylight hours. At Idul Adha animals are sacrificed and the meat is given to the poor. The Ascension of Mohammed and the Birthday of Mohammed are also national holidays, as are the Christian Ascension of Christ and Waisak, when Buddhists from all over the country gather at the Borobudur and Mendut temples to commemorate the birth and death of Buddha.

In addition to these national holidays, every region has its own local holidays, often cause for great celebration and festivity. In Bali the festivals of Galungan and Kuningan make up a 10-day celebration at the end of every Balinese calendar year (210 days). Shrines and temples are decorated, and music and dance performances are held.

For information on local festivities, consult the *Calendar of Events* published every year by the Directorate-General of Tourism, Jl. Kramat Raya 81, P.O. Box 409, Jakarta.

Flora and Fauna

Indonesia has tropical rain forests, black and white sand beaches, dormant and active volcanoes and fantastic marine life. There are orang-utans, Sumatran rhinos, tigers and elephants. Alas, most tourists will see these animals only in the zoo, especially well worth visiting in Jakarta and Surabaya.

Indonesia's nature reserves on most of the islands are undeveloped and accommodation, if any, is rustic. Nearly all reserves must be explored on foot, or on horseback where available. Access is often by sea or river rather than by road.

Leaflets on each of the reserves are available from the Directorate of Nature Conservation and Wildlife Management, called PPA (Direktorat Perlindungan dan Pengawetan Alam), at Jl. Juanda 9, Bogor, West Java. Written permits to enter the reserves must be obtained from PPA. There is also a book called *Nature Conservation in Indonesia* by Wendy Veevers-Carter, published in 1978 by PT Intermasa, Jakarta, for the World Wildlife Fund. This books lists all the major reserves and how to get there.

Even those who stay close to the beaten path will enjoy Indonesia's tropical plants—palms, frangipani, bougainvillea, hibiscus and lilies.

Photography

There's no better place to take pictures. Kodak and Fuji colour film are widely available in most larger cities. Prices are relatively high, however, and don't forget to check the expiry date. The best light for photography is from 7 to 10am and 3 to 5pm. Use a skylight filter to reduce the bluish haze at midday. Make sure to compensate for the bright sunlight, which tends to underexpose the subject.

Food and Drink

In big hotels and city restaurants Indonesian, Chinese and Western dishes are available. In Jakarta Thai, Mexican, Korean and Japanese cuisines are also represented. Make sure to try some Indonesian dishes, among them: *gado-gado* (a salad of parboiled green beans, soya beans and potatoes covered with a rich, tangy peanut sauce), *martabak* (a type of egg pancake stuffed with meat and vegetables), *mie goreng* (fried noodles with vegetables and meat), *nasi goreng* (spicy fried rice with vegetables and meat), *soto ayam* (chicken soup), *sate* (small pieces of barbecued meat, chicken or seafood roasted on a skewer over a charcoal fire), *bubur ayam* (chicken-rice porridge popular for breakfast), *opor ayam* (chicken in coconut milk), *rendang* (spicy beef) and *udang pete* (spicy prawns with a green vegetable that looks like a lima bean but has a strong flavour).

Complementing these main dishes are: *lumpia* (fried spring rolls), *acar* (a condiment of cucumber pickles), *krupuk* (giant shrimp chips), *emping* (small crisp chips made from *melinjo* seeds), *lontong* (rice cakes often served with *sate*), *sambal* (very spicy chilli sauce) and *kecap* (pronounced like 'ketchup' but actually soy sauce).

Fruits are not to be missed. Try **mango, papaya,** *nanas* (pineapple), *salak* (looks like a snake skin and is crunchy inside), *jeruk Bali* (a grapefruit without the bitterness), **rambutan** (red and hairy), **mangosteen** (brownish purple and hard-skinned with sweet white segments inside), *duku* (like little potatoes with sweet flesh inside) and **durian** (large greenish-brown with hard spines on the skin. You either love it or loathe it).

When buying drinks on the street, stick to name-brand bottled drinks

Market in Bukittinggi, West Sumatra

without ice. At your hotel or a clean-looking restaurant try *air jeruk panas* (hot, fresh lime soda), *es apokat* (a very sweet coconut milk drink with avocado), *es kelapa muda* (young coconut juice with soft globs of coconut) and good locally brewed beers (Bir Bintang, Anker and San Miguel; just ask for *'bir dingin'* — cold beer).

Sweets are usually available at hotel buffets or at counters in bakeries or big grocery stores. They are made of sticky rice often flavoured with brown palm sugar and sometimes wrapped in a banana leaf. Ask for *klepon,* delicious sticky rice balls with liquid brown sugar inside. Available in grocery stores in clear plastic packages are a good locally produced peanut brittle and sweet sesame wafers.

Etiquette

The people you'll meet will generally be very pleasant. A smile and gracious manners will go a long way to make your stay an enjoyable one. If a problem arises, stay calm and discuss the problem slowly. If your parents ever told you that patience is a virtue, now is the time to remember their words. Raised eyebrows, tapping feet and other signs of annoyance may seem to make things happen faster, but they leave a bad feeling behind.

Pass money and food with your right hand — the left is used for bathroom duties; don't point with your forefinger, don't crook your forefinger when summoning someone and don't pat children on the head. See the *Religion* section in the introduction for tips on visiting places of worship.

Suggested Reading

In Jakarta books can be purchased in hotel lobby bookstands (good selection at the Sari Pacific Hotel) and at Gunung Agung bookstores. One is at Jl. Kwitang 6, Menteng, Tel. 354563. Another is on the third floor of Ratu Plaza, Jl. Jend. Sudirman, Tel. 711649.

Before arriving in Indonesia, purchase books at the bookstores in the Singapore Airport transit and departure hall. There is also a small selection at the Jakarta Airport departure lounge. In Bali, the Hyatt and Bali Beach hotels both have good selections, as does Murni's Warung in Ubud, Bali. The main point to remember is that you should buy the book you want the moment you see it as distribution is spotty. Prices are high.

Informative guidebooks to complement the one you are reading this minute are the *Java, Bali* and *Indonesia* guidebooks published by APA Productions. *Historical Sites of Jakarta* by Adolf Heuken, a Jesuit priest and long-time Jakarta resident, puts together mountains of interesting detail about still-existing historical buildings and the people who inhabited them.

The enterprising members of the American Women's Association of Jakarta (Tel. 715172) have published *Introducing Indonesia* (primarily for expatriates living in Jakarta, but helpful for travellers around Indonesia too), *Indonesian Words and Phrases* (very handy) and *Jakarta Market* (with clear drawings and text explaining what all the exotic things in the markets are). Proceeds of these informative books go to Indonesian charities.

Oxford University Press publishes *Borobudur* by Jacques Dumarcay and *Bali* by Miguel Covarrubias, which first appeared in 1937 and is *the* classic on Balinese life. Personal accounts of life in Indonesia can be found in Oxford's *House in Bali* by musicologist Colin McPhee, *Coolie* by Madelon Lulofs and *Tale of Bali* by Vicky Baum. A fictional account of real-life Jakarta during the Sukarno days is found in *Twilight in Jakarta* by Mochtar Lubis, a top Indonesian writer.

One woman's experience of peacetime Bali and her participation in the struggle for Indonesian independence is the tale of *Revolt in Paradise* by K'tut Tantri.

The key figure behind the development of modern Balinese art is the subject of *Walter Spies and Balinese Art* by Hans Rhodius and John Darling.

A treasure-house of photos make up the coffee-table book *Indonesians: Portrait of an Archipelago* by Ian Charles Stewart and Judith Shaw. Former Singaporean Ambassador to Indonesia Lee Khoon Choy gives a highly personalised account of his diplomatic travels in *Indonesia Between Myth and Reality*.

To gain insight into the charismatic first president of Indonesia, read *The Smiling General* by O.G. Roeder, *Sukarno: An Autobiography* as told to Cindy Adams and *Sukarno: My Friend* by Cindy Adams. *Aspects of Indonesian Culture: Java and Sumatra* is a little handbook to the ethnography section of the National Museum. And last, but not least, is *Letters of a Javanese Princess*, written at the turn of the century by the national heroine Kartini.

Jakarta

Jakarta's new touch of class will surprise anyone who groaned over a visit to the city ten or twenty years ago. Today there's a veneer of international-style glamour. Banks and embassies flaunt experimental architecture, and highrise office towers with mirrored walls flank the main arteries of Jalan Rasuna Said and Jalan Jenderal Sudirman. Five-star hotels offer executive business centres, orchid-filled lobbies and caviar and smoked salmon on the menu. The museum at Taman Mini Indonesia Park is a sparkling, airconditioned showcase of Indonesia's traditional culture. Shopping centres like Ratu Plaza offer today's consumer everything from crystal chandeliers to computer-graphics T-shirts. Well-stocked supermarkets purvey French champagne, Japanese seaweed and Scandinavian biscuits.

Happily, however, Jakarta has not been modernised or sanitised into international homogeneity. It's still a city with humanity and interest, with quirks and contrasts to intrigue and annoy its residents and visitors. On the road you'll see ambassadors and businessmen nestled in the back seats of their chauffeur-driven cars while next to them one man balances his bicycle laden with fifty live chickens tied to the handlebars, and another man herds a water buffalo to market.

Elsewhere in Jakarta is the City Hall, which most of the time looks like an office building anywhere in the world—its lobby large, bare and marble. But at midday on Friday take another look. The City Hall lobby becomes an enormous mosque for hundreds of government workers kneeling in prayer on rugs and newspaper pages. Elsewhere in the city white-uniformed salesgirls sell modern antibiotics in brightly-lit drugstores, while outside a sarong-clad '*jamu* lady' sells traditional herbal medicines that can shake a cold, improve circulation and eliminate unsightly pimples.

The people have worked hard to make Jakarta a national capital of significance. Enormous colour portraits of visiting world leaders regularly appear in front of the swank Mandarin Hotel. Local entrepreneurs, foreign bankers, government ministers and oil executives work hand in hand in the vigorous business centre. Students strive for places in the prestigious University of Indonesia. At Pertamina Hospital staff are learning to use up-

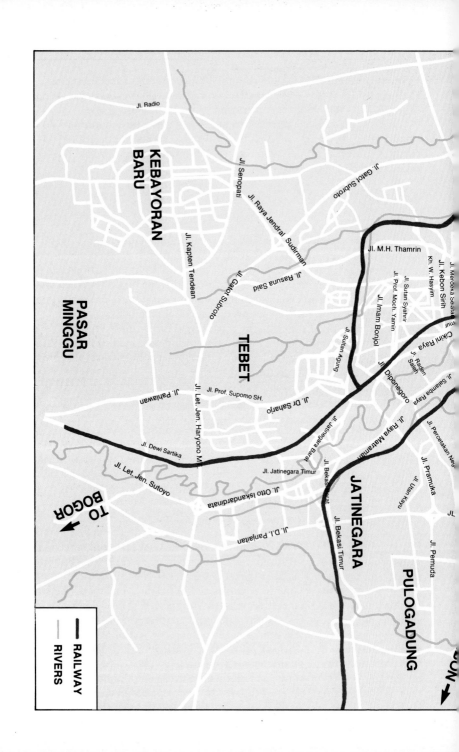

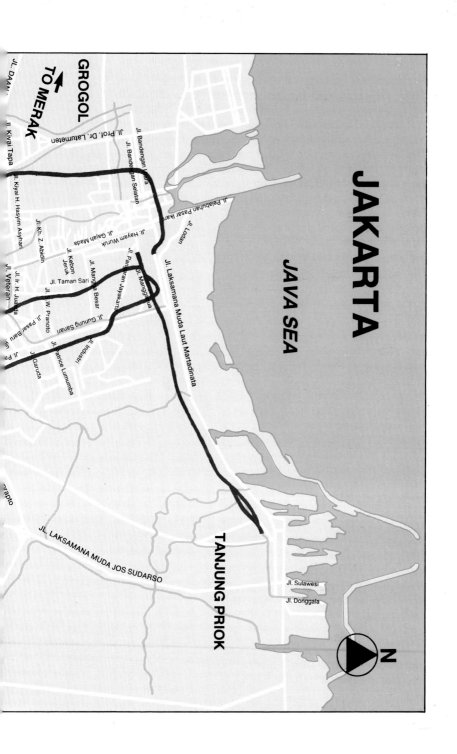

to-date diagnostic and clinical equipment. Government servants pore over endless studies and reports on national development. It is here that President Suharto maintains his official residences, the Istana Negara (the State Palace) and the Istana Merdeka (Freedom Palace).

Jakarta's seven million people live and work in a great variety of places: temporary shacks along the railway tracks, neat cinderblock homes and spacious airconditioned villas. Throughout the city are *kampungs*, pockets of one-storey homes tightly packed together where neighbours greet one another on paved paths surrounded by playing children and clucking chickens. Under the vast government system that begins at the top with the governor of Jakarta, down to the elected, unpaid *kampung* chief, things are improving all the time. Where power cuts once were, they are no more. Where gas lamps once lit homes, electricity lights children's homework. Jakarta straddles the old and the new, providing a wealth of contrasting sights for the visitor.

History

Jakarta is not a new city. In fact its history goes as far back as the 5th century AD when it was a settlement of the Hindu kingdom of Taruma Negara. Known as Sunda Kelapa, the settlement grew to become a thriving harbour town of 10,000 people. In 1527 the Muslims, led by Fatahillah, conquered the city, giving it the name Jayakarta, meaning 'Perfect Victory', the name on which Jakarta is based.

At the beginning of the 17th century Dutch traders came to Jayakarta and overthrew the indigenous people, setting up the city of Batavia. At first Batavia was a walled city, to protect the Dutch from the wild animals that roamed the countryside as well as from the local people, who were not pleased about the arrival of the foreign newcomers. The Dutch built themselves a city hall, town square and church in the area known today as Kota (literally meaning 'City').

As the Dutch became more firmly entrenched, their city grew southwards, where they built government buildings, the National Museum and the palaces that are today the official residence of President Suharto. While the Menteng area is the so-called city centre, Jakarta has continued to spread southwards since the Declaration of Independence in 1945, and today it is a sprawling national capital which is constantly being improved and developed.

Embassies

Fifty-three countries have diplomatic missions or representatives in Jakarta. Among them are the embassies of:

Australia	Jl. Thamrin 15. Tel. 323109
Canada	Wisma Metropolitan, Jl. Sudirman. Tel. 514022

France	Jl. Thamrin 20. Tel. 332807
Great Britain	Jl. Thamrin 75. Tel. 330904
India	Jl. Rasuna Said. Tel. 518150
Japan	Jl. Thamrin 24. Tel. 324308
Malaysia	Jl. Imam Bonjol 17. Tel. 332170
Netherlands	Jl. Rasuna Said. Tel. 511515
New Zealand	Jl. Diponegoro 41. Tel. 330552
Philippines	Jl. Imam Bonjol 6-8. Tel. 348917
Singapore	Jl. Proclamasi 23. Tel. 348761
Thailand	Jl. Imam Bonjol 74. Tel. 343762
United States	Jl. Medan Merdeka Selatan 5. Tel. 360360
West Germany	Jl. Thamrin 1. Tel. 323908.

Airlines

Twenty-three international airlines have representative offices in Jakarta. Those with direct service to Jakarta are:

Cathay Pacific	Hotel Borobudar. Tel. 3806660
China Airlines	Jl. Gajah Mada 3-5. Tel. 353193
Garuda	Nusantara Building. Tel. 333408
Japan Airlines	President Hotel. Tel. 322207
KLM	Hotel Indonesia. Tel. 320708
Lufthansa	Panin Centre. Tel. 710247
MAS	Hotel Indonesia. Tel. 320909
Philippines Airlines	Hotel Borobudur. Tel. 370108
Qantas	BDN Building. Tel. 326707
Singapore Airlines	Sahid Jaya Hotel. Tel. 5780873
Swissair	Hotel Borobudur. Tel. 373608
Thai International	BDN Building. Tel. 320607
UTA	Jaya Building. Tel. 323507

Sightseeing

Getting Around. For the tourist, Jakarta has a lot to offer. Because things are scattered over wide distances, the visitor with only a few days would probably do best taking one of the city tours offered by tour operators located in hotel lobbies. Two of the big agencies are Pacto (Hotel Borobudar Tel. 356952) and Nitour (2 Jl. Majapahit, Tel. 346344). Alternatively, taxis are available in front of big hotels, can be flagged down on the street or summoned by telephone (Blue Bird Taxi, Tel. 325607, 334397). All taxis have meters (make sure they are turned on) and fares are moderate. Blue Bird taxis and cars are also available by the hours (US$7 for two hours, unairconditioned; $8-$11 for two hours, airconditioned).

Public buses are not recommended as they are crowded and the drivers

do not speak English. To get around on your own, use the excellent Falk street map of Jakarta, available at local bookstands for about US$8. The Jakarta Visitor Information Centre is in the Jakarta Theatre Building, Jalan Thamrin 9. Tel. 354094, 364093. When sightseeing start early. By midday it's hot. During the rainy season there are usually clear skies in the morning, showers in the afternoon.

Though willing, people on the street may not be able to communicate helpful directions to the lost tourist. Make sure your valuables are safely stored in the hotel safe deposit box, and hang on tightly to your purse.

Kota

An interesting place to begin your tour of Jakarta is in Kota, the oldest part of town, located on the northern coast of the city. To the north of Kota is the historic port **Pasar Ikan** and the Dutch colonial area around **Taman Fatahillah.** To the south of Kota is **Glodok,** or Chinatown. A full day can easily be spent in the Kota area, although it is hot and exhausting due to the congestion of the area. Less stressful is a city bus tour of its highlights.

Kota can be reached from Merdeka Square on the main road heading north, Jalan Gajah Mada. It is separated by a canal (an artery of transport in early Jakarta days) from Jalan Majapahit, which you will take back to your hotel at the end of your Kota tour.

On your way to Kota notice the historic buildings along Jalan Gajah Mada. The **National Archives Building** at number 111 is a fine example of the Dutch colonial houses which formerly used to fill the area. Don't miss the **Chinese community centres** with their peaked roofs which once housed the eminent leaders of the Chinese community in Jakarta's earlier days. Further on, just before you reach Taman Fatahillah you will see the Kota **railway station** built by the Dutch in art deco style, and the **Bank Indonesia,** another former colonial building.

You'll soon reach Taman Fatahillah, or **Fatahillah Square,** named after the Muslim leader who conquered Jakarta in 1527. Three sides of the square house museums and on the fourth is a two-storey, picturesque restaurant where you can relax over a cool drink.

On one side of the square is the **Jakarta City Museum,** or **Museum Sejarah Jakarta** (open 9am-2.30pm Tuesday-Thursday; 9am-noon Friday; 9am-1pm Saturday and 9am-3pm Sunday, Tel. 679101). This handsome former city hall was built in 1710 and today displays antique furniture, maps, paintings and other memorabilia of Jakarta's history. In the basement are dismal dungeons.

On another side of the square is the cool, white neo-classical **Ceramics Museum (Museum Keramik)** at Jalan Taman Fatahillah 2 (hours: 9am-2pm daily, Tel. 671060). Inside is the fine ceramics collection of former Vice President Adam Malik. Also located in this building is the **Museum of Fine**

Arts or **Balai Seni Rupa** (open 9am-2pm daily, Tel. 676090). Look for works by Indonesia's finest painters, beginning with the 19th century artist Raden Saleh, who attracted attention in the salons of Europe. Also note works by Hendra, Sadali, Basuki Abdullah and Sudjoyono.

On the third side of the square is the charming little **Wayang Museum** at Jalan Pintu Besar Utara 27 (hours: 9am-2pm Tuesday-Thursday and Sunday; 9am-1pm Saturday, Tel. 679560). Notice the *wayang kulit* (flat leather puppets), *wayang golek* (three-dimensional doll-like puppets) and *wayang klitik* (flat wooden puppets).

From Taman Fatahillah take a five-minute taxi ride to the coastal area known as **Pasar Ikan** (meaning 'fish market'). Most colourful here is the wharf where tall-masted sailing ships unload timber from the outer islands and stock up on everything from motorcycles to rubber sandals. To enter the wharf area, pay a small entrance fee at the toll-gate. Once on the wharf you can walk up and down (great photo opportunities) or hire a little boat whose helmsman will glide you along the wharfside for about Rps 1,000 for half an hour.

Standing on the wharf, look past the ships and slightly to the left and you will see the historic **watchtower** at Jalan Ikan, once used by the Dutch to patrol the port. For a small fee you can climb to the top of the watchtower and look over the entire port area. Down below you will see the **Museum Bahari,** a rather disappointing maritime museum housed in the original warehouses of the Dutch East India Company. Across from the museum is a fascinating market loaded with shells.

Driving back to the central area of town, stop off at the **Gereja Sion** at 1 Jalan Pangeran Jayakarta, called the Portuguese Church for the original Portuguese and Eurasian parish. Inside are a pipe organ with hand-cranked bellows, and a baroque pulpit and organ loft. This is the oldest existing church in Jakarta.

Continue south to the Chinatown area of **Glodok,** where there is a **Chinese temple** or *klenteng* on a back street off Jalan Gajah Mada. The temple complex itself is a peaceful oasis. Known as the Temple of Golden Virtue, it was built in about 1650 and is a focal point of the community where people shake fortune-telling sticks, light tall red votive candles and burn incense as they pray.

Jakarta Pusat

The **National Monument,** called Monas (short for Monumen Nasional), is the logical place to start a tour of Jakarta Pusat, the central part of Jakarta where offices, banks, government buildings, the presidential palaces, hotels, museums and churches happily coexist. Monas (open daily 9am-5pm except the last Monday of each month. Entrance fee Rps 200) is the tall thin monument topped by a golden flame in the centre of the large

Merdeka Square. In the basement is a small museum with 48 diaramas showing the history of Indonesia from prehistoric man through the Hindu-Buddhist period up to the present. In the Hall of Contemplation is a replica of the Proclamation of Independence. Take the elevator ride to the lookout platform at the top and see the vast panorama of the city.

From Monas take a very short taxi ride or walk over to the west side of Merdeka Square to the **National Museum** (Jl. Merdeka Barat 12, Tel. 360976. Open Tuesday, Wednesday, Thursday and Sunday from 8.30am to 3pm; Friday from 8.30 to 11am and Saturday from 8.30am to 1.30pm. Closed Monday). Catch one of the very informative English guided tours given by the Ganesha Volunteers on Tuesday, Wednesday and Thursday at 9.30am. See the *History and Culture* section in the Introduction (page 10) for details on the museum's collection. On the ground floor visit the ethnography section showing implements of everyday life, the stone section of Hindu and Buddhist sculpture, the prehistory section with Java Man's skull and the ceramics section, said to be the most important collection in Southeast Asia.

Upstairs don't miss the bronze room (with outstanding sculptures of Shiva and Prajnaparamita) and, open only on Sundays, the gold treasure room. On Sunday morning you may be lucky enough to see a *gamelan* performance in the courtyard. Under the stairs of the front hall is a little shop with a small collection of Indonesian handicrafts and books on Indonesian art and culture.

After the museum, catch a taxi and drive clockwise around the square. On the north side you will see the palace grounds holding the **Istana Merdeka** (Freedom Palace) and the **Istana Negara** (State Palace), once the homes of the Dutch governors-general and now the official presidential residence. They are only open by special advance appointment.

Continue on to the **Istiqlal Mosque** (Jalan Veteran), the largest mosque in Asia. To enter just park your shoes at the reception desk and climb up to the enormous prayer hall. Across the street visit the well-preserved neo-Gothic **Roman Catholic Cathedral**, Jalan Cathedral 7, completed at the start of this century.

Continue your swing around the area via Jalan Medan Merdeka Utara, where you will see the **Gereja Emmanuel**, Jalan Merdeka Timur 10, a circular church built in 1835 for use by Dutch Protestants and, a little further on, the Indonesian **Petroleum Club**, a private club once the home of the head of Royal Dutch Shell.

Bear right on to Jalan Medan Merdeka Selatan past the **American Embassy** and the **Jakarta City Hall** and you have completed your tour around Merdeka Square. Continue southwards a few minutes along Jalan Thamrin, where you will see the headquarters of the big banks and businesses, the United Nations and **Sarinah's Department Store**. Have lunch in the coffee shop of the Mandarin or Sari Pacific Hotel.

After lunch continue your drive from Jalan Thamrin eastwards on **Jalan Imam Bonjol,** known as Embassy Row, noting the especially beautiful American ambassador's residence at the corner of Taman Suropati (where the governor of Jakarta also lives) and further on the elegant Egyptian ambassador's residence. Finish your Jakarta Pusat tour with shopping at the **Jalan Surabaya** flea market.

Taman Mini Indonesia Indah

Well worth your while is a half-day trip to **Taman Mini** (Beautiful Indonesia in Miniature Park). Open from 9am to 5pm, it is a 120-acre cultural park located in east Jakarta near Halim airport, about a 30-minute drive from the centre of town. You can take a bus tour there or take a taxi. Private guides are available at the information office.

Included within the park are full-scale replicas of the architecturally distinctive regional homes of Indonesia. There is an excellent museum of Indonesian arts and crafts in the large, Balinese-style building to the left as you enter (not well marked, but very interesting). Bird lovers will enjoy the domed aviary. You can walk around the park yourself or take the little park train, open-sided tram or aerial cable car. Cool off with a real coconut from one of the cold drink stands in the park. Empty on weekdays and crowded on Sundays.

Other Areas of Jakarta

Jakarta has many other interesting areas, but because they are widely scattered they are only mentioned briefly here. The **Textile Museum,** Jalan Tuban 4 (open 9am-2pm Tuesday to Sunday, Tel. 365367) displays traditional Indonesian textiles.

The Satriamandala **Armed Forces Museum** (Museum Abri) on Jalan Gatot Subroto (opposite the Kartika Chandra Hotel) is open from 8am to 3pm Tuesday-Sunday, Tel. 582759. It is a military museum displaying weapons, antique planes and diaramas highlighting Indonesia's struggle for independence.

In the Kebayoran area to the south of the city you'll see luxurious homes, the picturesque white **Al-Azhar Mosque** on Jalan Pattimura, the new ASEAN Secretariat building designed in receding sections to look like rice terraces, the **flower and bird markets** at Jalan Barito, and the **Blok M** shopping centre.

There are **orchid gardens (Taman Anggrek)** in the middle of the Senayan Sports Complex and at the Taman Anggrek Indonesia Permai, a 35,000 square metre area in the Slipi section.

Shopping

Shopping is a highlight of a visit to Jakarta, especially when looking for arts and crafts from the far-flung reaches of Indonesia.

Batik, Arts and Crafts: Most hotel lobbies have shopping arcades. If you have time for only one stop make it the third floor of Sarinah's Department Store, Jl. M.H. Thamrin 11, Menteng, open from 9.30am to 5.30pm Monday through Saturday. It is loaded with handicrafts: silver, batik, pewter, leather, tortoiseshell, baskets and paintings all at reasonable, fixed prices. Also try their branch store: Sarinah Jaya, Jl. Iskandarsyah II/2, Kebayoran Baru, near Blok M. It is more modern, but has a smaller selection. Open daily from 9am to 9pm.

A side street leading away from Blok M shopping centre is called Jalan Palatehan. Here you'll find several shops selling antiques, handicrafts, batik and locally-made toys. The most elegant is Hadiprana Galleries (Jl. Palatehan I/38) with a nice ground floor art gallery of modern Indonesian paintings and distinctive note cards. Other shops on the street are Pigura Arts (at No.41) and Pura Art Shop (at No.43).

There is a nice selection of crafts, especially Balinese ones, at Banuwati (Java Boutique), Jl. Semarang 14, Menteng.

The following stores specialise in batik only and sell shirts, dresses, place mats, wall hangings and cushions: Batik G.K.B.I. (Jl. Jend. Sudirman 28, close to the Hilton, a co-operative of batik manufacturers), Srikandi Batik Shop (Jl. Melawai VI/6A, Kebayoran Baru), Batik Danar Hadi (1A Jl. Raden Saleh, Tel. 342390, popular with the elite of Jakarta) and the really special P.T. Ramacraft (Jl. Panarukan 25, Menteng and Borobudur Hotel). This shop is owned by Jakarta's leading batik designer, Iwan Tirta, and is a must on every VIP ladies' tour of Jakarta.

Antiques: Indonesia's lovely antiques include Chinese and European-style carved furniture, traditional textiles, kris (Javanese ceremonial daggers) and Chinese ceramics. So that you can visit several shops at once, they are listed by area. In Kebayoran Baru are Tony's Gallery (Jl. Wijaya XIII/45, Specialises in antique furniture, lamps, textiles, porcelain and bronzes) and Madjapahit Art and Curio (Jl. Melawai III/4, Blok M).

In the Menteng area visit Alex and Caecil Papadimitriou, Jl. Pasaruan 3. They have a wide range of antiques and will refinish the furniture to your specifications. Ask to see their high-quality collection of modern Indonesian paintings by appointment. Other Menteng antique stores are Djody (Jl. Kebon Sirih Timur Dalam 22) and Nasrun (Jl. Kebon Sirih Timur Dalam 39). Also check the other antique stores on this small street. Johan's is at Jalan Wahid Hasyim 80.

Also in Menteng is the legendary Jalan Surabaya, a street lined with stalls jammed with junk and treasures of all sorts—opium scales, blowguns, brassware, clocks, furniture—you name it. Great ceramic finds if you know what you are doing; terrible rip-offs if you don't. Don't believe a word you hear from the salesmen, and bargain with all your might.

In the Kota area are Garuda Arts (Jl. Majapahit 12), Lee Cheong (Jl.

Majapahit 32) and **Polim** (Jl. Gajah Mada 126)

Jewellery: Beadwork, silver, tortoiseshell and semi-precious stone jewellery can be found at Sarinah's Department Store, listed above. Nice silver jewellery with a modern look using traditional Indonesian motifs is available at Linda **Spiro** (Borobudur Hotel), Joyce Spiro (Sari Pacific Hotel) and F. Spiro (Hilton Hotel bazaar). Buy Indonesian opals at **Pelangi** in the Hilton Hotel bazaar.

Pasars: If you want to see how most of Jakarta shops, visit a *pasar*. Pasar **Blok M** is a good one to see if you enjoy crowds. It is a large bazaar several blocks wide that includes a four-storey modern shopping centre called Aldiron Plaza and more traditional fruit and vegetable stands as well as cramped little stalls selling anything you could imagine. As you wander around you will see opal salesmen, counters offering traditional herbal medicines, handcrafted textiles and sports equipment. Stop for an ice cream at Gaston's on Jalan Melawai III/28 in Blok M.

Another fascinating *pasar* is **Pasar Mayestic,** which is also in Kebayoran, although this one is smaller and less overwhelming than Blok M.

Cassettes: Pirated cassettes are a booming business in Jakarta. In Aldiron Plaza, the modern building in the centre of Blok M, you'll find shops that are plentifully stocked with Western classical, jazz and rock along with Indonesian traditional and modern selections. The cassettes line the walls,

The National Mosque among the red tile roofs of Jakarta

Replica of a West Sumatran house at Taman Mini Indonesia Indah

and you're free to spend an hour or so listening to your choices at the rows of stereo headsets. Prices are around Rps 2,700 per cassette.

Hairdressers: For a chic haircut for men or women, call for an appointment at Rudy Salon in the Mandarin Hotel or at Ratu Plaza Shopping Centre, 2nd Floor, Jl. Jend. Sudirman.

Smocked Dresses: Adorable handmade confections for little girls at Yayasan Hasta Karya, Jl. Raden Saleh 52, Jakarta Pusat. Open 9am-2pm Monday to Saturday. Out of the way, but worth it if smocked dresses are your thing. Located in a tiny building off the parking lot across the street from the famous Oasis Restaurant.

Sports and Recreation

In the Hotels: The best bet for a tourist who is looking for recreation is to stay at a hotel with sports facilities. The Hilton Hotel offers its guests the use of its posh Executive Club with tennis courts (lighted at night), swimming in two pools, bowling, squash and jogging track. The Borobudur Hotel also offers a large pool, squash, tennis and jogging. Clark Hatch physical fitness centres are located in the Hilton and Mandarin hotels.

Bowling: Public bowling at the Kartika Chandra Bowling Centre at the Hotel Kartika Chandra on Jl. Gatot Subroto (open 9am to midnight) and at Kebayoran Bowl, Jl. Melawai IX, Blok M (open 10am to 11pm). There are bowling alleys for hotel guests at the Hilton Executive Club.

Golf: Public courses in Jakarta are well maintained and are open from sunrise to sunset (about 6.15pm). Less crowded on weekdays than on weekends. The best public courses, offering equipment rental, caddies, etc. are Ancol Golf Course (Taman Jaya Impian Ancol, Tel. 681511), Halim Golf Course (Jl. Halim Raya, Jakarta Timur, Tel. 800793), Kebayoran Golf Course (Jl. Asia-Afrika, Pintu IX, Senayan, Tel. 582508) and, about one hour's drive out of Jakarta in the town of Bogor, the beautiful Bogor Golf Course, Jl. Semeru, Bogor, Tel. Bogor 22891).

Diving: There is excellent diving off Jakarta's shores For further information see The Thousand Islands in the West Java section, page 61.

Ancol: Jakarta's largest recreation area is Taman Impian Jaya Ancol (Ancol Dreamland), which is in north Jakarta about 30 minutes from the city centre. Families can easily spend a whole day here taking in all the sights and activities. There is an 18-hole, international standard golf course and driving range open from 6am to 6pm.

Kids will love the swimming pool complex, which includes a huge wading pool, a 350-metre pool which looks like a jogging track filled with water that moves you along in a gentle current, a simulated wave pool, and a pool with five and ten-metre high slides. Beware of the slides. If you don't sit up straight you can pull your back, and if you bend your knees on hitting the water you are likely to slam your kneecap. (Yes, this is written from personal experience.)

There is also an Oceanarium with trained dolphin and sea-lion shows, and kiddie boat rides through this area. Make sure to visit the Pasar Seni, or Art Market, where local craftsmen are at work. Children like the playground area where there are go-karts for them to race in. There is a modern or traditional cultural show at Ancol every night and Sunday morning. Ask at your hotel for the schedule. Ancol is open daily, is quite empty during the week but busy on the weekends. The Ancol marina is the departure point for trips to the Thousand Islands.

Ragunan Zoo: A first-rate zoo known as Kebun Binatang Ragunan is located on Jalan Ragunan in Pasar Minggu and is open from 9am to 6pm daily. About 30 minutes from Jakarta's centre, it has a vast, natural setting in which the animals—monkeys, orang-utans, elephants, lions and hippos —are at home. Worth a trip.

Amusement Parks: Children five and up will enjoy Taman Ria Monas, an amusement park with carnival rides which is located at Merdeka Square. Open 5-11pm Monday to Saturday and 8am-11pm Sundays and holidays.

Smaller children will like Taman Ria Remaja, Jalan Pintu VII, Senayan, where there are rides for small children, pleasant grounds and a lake. Go between the 4pm opening and sunset. Open all day on Sunday.

Cultural Programmes

Look in the *Jakarta Post* to see what cultural programmes are on. Every night there is a performance at **Taman Ismail Marzuki**, or T.I.M., the Jakarta arts centre at Jalan Cikini Raya 73, Tel. 342605. This is a complex of indoor, outdoor and experimental theatres. Foreigners who don't speak Bahasa Indonesia can enjoy dance performances from throughout Indonesia. The quality of the performances varies considerably from world class to frankly amateur. Tickets are inexpensive and are usually available at the door. Occasionally there are dance and musical performances sponsored by foreign embassies.

At the Jakarta Hilton open-air **Balinese Theatre** there are hour-long performances nightly (except Monday) at 7pm of traditional dances accompanied by *gamelan* music. On Monday night there is a traditional *wayang kulit* performance. Lovely setting. Tickets at the door. Have a pizza afterwards at the pizzeria in the Hilton garden.

The Ganesha Volunteers present 16 **slide-lectures** per year, October to May, on aspects of Indonesian culture at the Erasmus Huis, the Dutch Cultural Centre on Jalan Rasuna Said in Kuningan, Tel. 512321.

There is a cultural show and dinner at the Borobudur Hotel every Friday night at 7pm held at the poolside. Price includes welcome drink. Call 370108 Ext. 2308 for reservations.

Wayang orang dance drama with flashy traditional costumes and *gamelan* is performed for a local audience every Tuesday, Wednesday, Friday and Sunday evening from 6.15pm until about midnight at the Bharata Theatre on Jalan Kalilio.

The **foreign cultural centres** occasionally offer public lectures and performances of interest. Check the *Jakarta Post*'s What's On section or phone ahead for information from the British Council (Widjoyo Centre, Jalan Jend. Sudirman 56, Tel. 587411) or the Erasmus Huis (Dutch Embassy, Jalan Rasuna Said, Kuningan, Tel. 512321).

Nightlife

Check the *Jakarta Post* for **film showings**. Theatres are usually airconditioned and tickets are cheap. Films may be in Bahasa Indonesia, with or without English subtitles. To see a colourful Indonesian-made movie (with lots of romance and daring) visit the pleasant movie theatre at the T.I.M. cultural centre.

Discotheques: The nicest discos are the Oriental Club at the Hilton Hotel (open to members and hotel guests. Lost of flashing lights and 'in-crowd' local singles) and the Pitstop at the Sari Pacific Hotel (non-members only on weekdays).

Nightclubs: A large Chinese-Indonesian nightclub with floorshow and Chinese meal is the Blue Ocean Restaurant and Nite Club at Jalan Hayam

Wayang kulit *puppets and* gamelan *instruments*

Wuruk 5, Tel. 361134. Western entertainment at the Nirwana Supper Club at the top of the Hotel Indonesia, Jalan Thamrin, Tel. 320008.

Bars: Luxurious surroundings and live background music are found at the Hilton Hotel's Kudus Bar and the Mandarin Hotel's Captain's Bar. There's a pub atmosphere at the Jaya Pub behind the Jaya Building on Jalan Thamrin, and at the George and Dragon, Jalan Telukbetung 32 off Jalan Thamrin. The latter is a popular place with young, single expatriates. The Bodega Grill (next to Galael Supermarket, Jalan Terogong Raya, Cilandak, Tel. 767798) presents country and western music on Friday nights, Dixieland on Saturdays and jazz on Sundays.

Hotels

Jakarta has hotels in all categories, with the five-star hotels matching luxury hotels anywhere in the world in service and style. All rates listed below are for double rooms. Add on 21 percent service and tax.

Five-Star Hotels

Jakarta Hilton
Jl. Gatot Subroto, Senayan
Tel. 583051; Telex 46673
US$105-$130.

Beautiful lobby modelled on a Javanese palace. Extensive grounds.
Complete sports facilities. Hotel guests get free use of Clark Hatch
gymnasium with several daily exercise classes. 423 rooms with new wing
under construction. Conveniently located between business and residential
areas. Japanese restaurant, pizzeria, Taman Sari grillroom.

Borobudur Inter-Continental
Jl. Lapangan Banteng Selatan
Jakarta Pusat
Tel. 370108; Telex 44156
$110.
Extensive grounds with enormous pool, squash, tennis and mini-
golf. Sunday jazz night in the Pendopo Bar. Japanese Keio restaurant, Toba
rotisserie and Malayan seafood restaurant. Popular coffee shop. Notice the
hotel's logo: not just concentric squares but the aerial view of the famous
Borobudur monument.

Jakarta Mandarin
Jl. M.H. Thamrin, Jakarta Pusat
Tel. 321307; Telex 45755
$123-$139.
504 rooms. Small pool. Clark Hatch fitness centre. A favourite with
businessmen and women who like the prime location in the central
business district. Club Room (grillroom), Spice Garden Szechuan
restaurant, Captain's Bar and coffee shop with tasty Asian dishes. On
Friday night try the Malam Kaki Lima, a poolside spread of typical
Indonesian *sate* and other snacks served from colourful local food carts
(Rps 6,000 per person). Spacious, luxurious bedrooms.

Four-Star Hotels

Sari Pacific
Jl. Thamrin 6, Jakarta Pusat
Tel. 323707; Telex 44514
$105-$111.
Top of the line four-star hotel. Pool. 500 rooms. Disco. Cheerful lobby and
good bakery where French matrons come in droves. Jayakarta grillroom
with salad bar and bread basket the size of a wheelbarrow. Furusato
Japanese restaurant. Excellent central location.

Sahid Jaya
Jl. Jenderal Sudirman
Tel. 587031; Telex 46331
Pool. 514 rooms. $75 double. Good Chinese seafood at Mina restaurant.

Hyatt Aryaduta
Jl. Perapatan 44-46
Tel. 376008; Telex 46220
235 rooms. $80 double. Newly redecorated Le Parisien restaurant and popular Japanese restaurant.

Hotel Indonesia
Jl. Thamrin
Tel. 320008; Telex 61233
666 rooms. $70 double. Pool. Nirwana supper club. Japanese restaurant. Central location. Oldest four-star hotel in town.

President
Jl. Thamrin 59
Tel. 320508; Telex 46724
354 rooms. $58-$72. Good Bangkay Japanese restaurant. Central. Popular with Japanese.

Three-Star Hotels

Kartika Chandra
Jl. Gatot Subroto
Tel. 511808; Telex 46470
175 rooms. $72. Movie theatre adjacent. Pool.

Kartika Plaza
Jl. M.H. Thamrin 10
Tel. 321008; Telex 45792
250 rooms, centrally located. $60.

Kemang
Jl. Kemang Raya
Kebayoran Baru
Tel. 793208; Telex 47243
100 rooms. $46. Out of the way but may be handy if visiting local residents. Pool.

Two-Star Hotels

Kebayoran Inn
Jl. Senayan 87
Tel. 716208
61 rooms. $22.

Sabang Palace
Jl. Setia Budi Raya 24
Tel. 514640; Telex 44555
41 rooms. Pool.

Council of Churches Guest House
Jl. Tenku Umar 17, Menteng
Tel. 342896
Not a rated hotel, but a small guest house with simple rooms in an old
Dutch colonial house. Share meals with other guests—Indonesian and
foreign.

Restaurants

As befits a capital city, Jakarta has restaurants of all types reflecting the
cosmopolitan tastes of its tourists and residents.

Indonesian
The **Sari Bundo** (Jl. Juanda 27, Tel. 358343) serves the best Padang food:
very hot spicy dishes piled on your table. You only pay for what you eat.
The rest is thrown back into the pot. Local atmosphere. Also try their
branch, the **Restaurant Famili** (Jl. Melawai IV, Blok M, Kebayoran). Both
are closed during the fasting month. The **Mirasari** (Jl. Patiunus 13,
Kebayoran Baru, Tel. 771621) is informal. Eat inside or on the garden
terrace.

The **Sate House Senayan** is a chain of pleasant, informal restaurants
serving excellent sizzling-hot *sate* and other local dishes tastily prepared.
Restaurants are located at Jalan Pakubuwono VI/6 (Tel. 715821), Jalan
Kebon Sirih 31A (Tel. 326238) and Jalan Cokroaminoto 78 (Tel. 344248).

Mixed
The modern Ratu Plaza shopping centre on Jalan Sudirman houses
several nice restaurants offering differing types of food. They are the **House
of Pangeran** (Tel. 711333. Indonesian and Western food. Javanese palace
decor), **Raffles Tavern** (Tel. 711894. Western pub-style), **New Hama** (Tel.
713173. Japanese teppanyaki steakhouse). On the third floor there is a sushi
bar and a quick Indonesian-style cafeteria. In the basement try **Kentucky
Fried Chicken** and **Swensen's** Ice Cream Parlour.

Chinese
The **Spice Garden** in the Mandarin Hotel and the **Mina Seafood**
restaurant in the Sahid Jaya Hotel are both good. **Yan Nyan** (Jl. Datu Ceper
69, off Jl. Hayam Wuruk, Tel. 364063) has excellent seafood at moderate
prices. Reservations advised. **Ratu Bahari** (Jl. Melawai VIII/4, Kebayoran
Baru, Tel. 774115) is moderately priced though smoky and crowded.

Elegant Western
The Mandarin, Hilton, Hyatt, Borobudur and Sari Pacific hotels serve
excellent Western food in their grillrooms. The **Oasis** (Jl. Raden Saleh 47,
Tel. 327818) is a Jakarta legend set in a historic house loaded with
Indonesian arts and antiques. Sumatran Batak singers joyously fill the
dining room with song. Expensive.

Women working on a West Java tea plantation

Other Western

The **Ponderosa** (Ground Floor, Widjoyo Centre, Jl. Sudirman 57, Tel. 582823) is popular with local and expatriate families. Pleasant, informal atmosphere, good salad bar and tasty Mexican, Italian and Western food. **Ristorante Rugantino** (Jl. Melawai Raya 28, Kebayoran, Tel. 714727) has nice decor and Italian food. **Club Noordwijk** (Jl. Juanda 5A, Tel. 353909) is decorated with historical photos of Jakarta in days gone by. Indonesian buffet at lunch. **Swiss Inn** (Tel. 583280, Arthaloka Building, Jl. Sudirman) has Swiss atmosphere and fondues. The **Green Pub** (Jakarta Theatre Building, Jl. Thamrin 9, Tel. 325808) has a casual atmosphere, Margaritas, Mexican food and a cowboy band at night.

Japanese

Try the expensive restaurants at the Jakarta Hilton, the Borobudur, the President and the Hyatt hotels. More moderate and less fancy are **Kobe** (Jl. Blora 27, Tel. 356780 and **Kikugawa** (Jl. Kebon Binatang III/13, Tel. 327198). It's a little out of the way. Small and informal but nice atmosphere. Only airconditioning is in the private tatami rooms.

Other Asian

Korean food at **Koreana** (Jl. Melawai VI/3, Blok M, Tel. 713776) and at **New Korean House** (Jl. Thamrin next to Asoka Hotel, Tel. 322908). **Omar Khayyam** (Jl. Antara 5-7, Pasar Baru, Tel. 356719) is Jakarta's only Indian

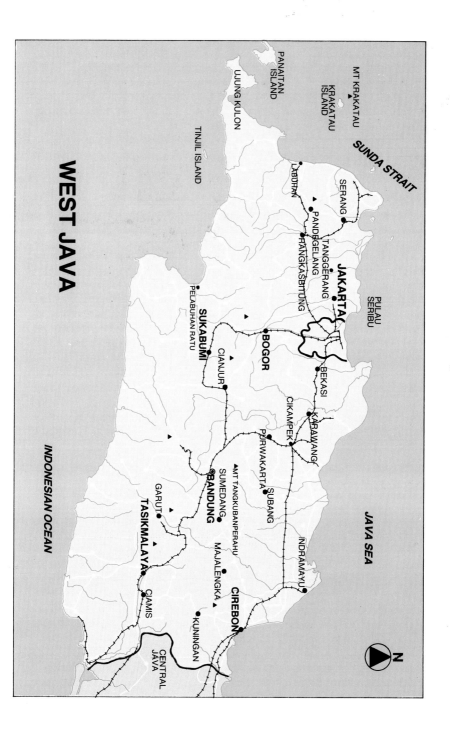

restaurant. Good buffet lunch. In seedy area. **Sri Thai Restaurant,** Setiabudi Building II, Jl. Rasuna Said, Kuningan is a nice new Thai restaurant, as is **D'jit Pochana** (Ground Floor, Complex Kehutanan, across from Bank Dagang Negara, Jl. Gatot Subroto, Tel. 581784. At this writing only open for lunch).

West Java

Jakarta, the capital of Indonesia, sits in the province of West Java. Using Jakarta as a base you can take a day trip to the lush botanical gardens of Bogor and to the Puncak to see the mountain views and expansive tea plantations.

Overnight trips out of Jakarta go to the Thousand Islands (*Pulau Seribu*) with fantastic snorkelling and diving in coral gardens alive with hundreds of species of tropical fish. White sand beaches are perfect for walking, shelling or snoozing. Take a night or two to visit the beaches at Carita or Samudra, or take the train over deep gorges to the mountain town of Bandung. Onward from Bandung is the city of Cirebon, which lies on the border of West and Central Java and is known for its colourful port and history as a centre of an Islamic kingdom.

West Javanese music is distinctive. In a cassette shop ask for a tape of the Sundanese (the area of West Java is called Sunda) *degung* music, with the alluring sound of the *suling* (flute) and the *kecapi* zither. At a hotel cultural show you'll see the *angklung*, a set of bamboo instruments. Because each of the instruments only makes one note on the scale, the *angklung* is played by a team of people, each shaking out the sound of a single note.

Bogor

Bogor is a good destination for a day trip from Jakarta. It can be reached in 45 minutes on the modern new Jagarawi toll highway. Jakarta travel agents such as Tunas in the Hilton Hotel offer day trips to Bogor for about US$20 per head including lunch. Located in the foothills of Puncak's volcanic peaks, Bogor is famous for its beautiful **Botanical Gardens.** The gardens cover 110 hectares and were founded in 1816. There are towering trees, paved pathways for strolling and an orchid house with English-speaking guide. Set within the garden is the **Presidential Palace** built by the Dutch governor-general in 1745 and restored in 1832. Open only by advance reservation. Just outside the gardens is a **Zoological Museum** that contains stuffed species of Indonesian fauna and 120,000 volumes of rare scientific books.

Don't miss the **gong factory** of Bapak Sukarna at Jalan Pancasan 17, a residential area not far from the town centre. Ask for the *bengkel gong* (gong factory). Here, in a shed with an earthen floor, you will marvel at a team of gongsmiths creating enormous gongs out of lumps of burning hot metal. Pak Sukarna's is the last factory in West Java to make the metal instruments you will recognise as part of the *gamelan* orchestra.

Restaurants in Bogor: The Orchid at Salak Hotel and Bogor Permai at Jalan Sudirman 15. Or have a picnic from your hotel in the Botanical Gardens.

Puncak

After visiting Bogor you can return to Jakarta for the night or continue up the mountain to the Puncak. The Puncak is a general name meaning summit and refers to the towns on the mountain hillsides south of Bogor. Jakarta's residents flock here on weekends to stay in the little guest houses and bungalows on either side of the main road up the mountain and to enjoy the cool evening air. Sweaters are advisable. There are long panoramic views up and down the mountains, and walks in the tea plantations.

Puncak hotels include the Puncak Pass Hotel (★★ 45 rooms, Jl. Raya Puncak, Sindanglaya, Cianjur, Tel. 2503. Bungalows in a pretty setting right at the pass with pool and tennis) and Evergreen (★★ Jl. Raya Puncak, Tugu, Tel. 4075). Both have restaurants for day trippers. While you are staying in the Puncak, put out the word that you want a pony ride (Rps 1,500 per hour) or that you would like antiques, and before you know it someone will appear leading a little pony or carrying a bundle filled with so-called 'antique' clocks, Dutch swords, *wayang golek* puppets, Dutch lamps and brass bowls.

Bandung

Bandung, the capital of West Java, lies on a plateau 187 kilometres south of Jakarta, 700 metres above sea level. You can reach Bandung in about four hours by car from Jakarta. If mountain driving, with its zigzags and hazardous situations, does not appeal to you, sit back and take the train. Tickets are available at Carnation Travel in Jakarta. You'll get a reserved seat cooled by an open window and a fan. The trip is scenic, a $3\frac{1}{4}$-hour ride over mountain gorges with country scenery. Soft drinks are available on the train. Bring a sandwich from your hotel.

Bandung gained fame in 1955 as the venue of the first Asian-African conference bringing together leaders of 29 nations to promote economic and cultural relations and take a common stand against colonialism.

You can get around Bandung by *becak*, although you'll probably hold your breath as the driver flies down the hill, dodging traffic. To take in all the sights, it is best to rent a car at your hotel, as the main sights are spread out. Up the hill from the centre of town is the **Institute of Technology** at Bandung (known as ITB), one of the nation's finest educational

institutions. Visit the **Textile Research Institute** and the **Ceramics Institute** together on Jalan Yani. At the Textile Institute the public relations staff will give you a tour of their factory, which makes everything from T-shirts to towels. At the Ceramics Institute you can see high quality reproductions of Chinese blue-and-white ceramics being made. Little to buy on the spot.

There are afternoon shows of local dancing and *angklung* music at Pak Udjo's Bamboo Workshop and Angklung School, Jalan Padasuka 118. Traditional **Sundanese dance** can be seen on Friday and Saturday nights at the Rumentang Siang, Jalan Baranang Siang 1; at the Grand Hotel Preanger, Jalan Asia-Afrika 81 every Friday night from 10pm to midnight; and at the Purwasetra, Jalan Oto Iskandardinata every night from 9pm. *Wayang golek* puppet shows are performed every Saturday night from 9am until dawn at the Yayasan Pusat Kebudayaan, Jalan Naripan 7.

Highlight of a trip to Bandung is a half-day trip out of town to the **Tangkubanperahu Volcano.** The volcano is an active one that last erupted in 1969. It is 15 kilometres from Bandung, and your driver can take you right up to the rim where the sulphur and steam pour out. There are guides to lead you on the three-hour hike into the crater. Wear strong shoes and be very careful you don't slip.

Seven kilometres past the volcano is the **Ciatur Hot Springs,** a resort where you can bathe in pools filled with steaming water. Too crowded on weekends. The ride is pretty through the tea plantations.

Bandung Hotels: Panghegar (★★★ 123 rooms. Jl. Merdeka 2, P.O. Box 506, Tel. 57751, Telex 28276) is a nice highrise building with a good coffee shop. Rooftop pool. The newest hotel in town is the Kumala Panghegar, Jl. Asia-Afrika 140 (★★★ Tel. 52141, P.O. Box 507, Telex 28276). The Savoy Homann (★★★ Jl. Asia-Afrika 112, P.O. Box 9, Tel. 58091).

Bandung Restaurants: Western and Indonesian dishes at the above hotels. Also try the Braga Permai, Jl. Braga. Tizi's on Jl. Dago has a garden setting and Western food. Queen's, Jl. Dalem Kaum 79, serves Chinese food.

For **shopping** for Indonesian arts and crafts, walk up and down Jalan Braga. The local **hospital** is the Adventist Hospital on Jalan Cihampelas, run by missionaries.

Cirebon

Continuing on from Bandung by car for 2½ hours you will come to Cirebon, which lies on the border of West and Central Java. It is a colourful seaport that was once the seat of an Islamic kingdom. The most revered of its past kings was the Sunan Gunung Jati, who was one of nine religious leaders to spread Islam in Indonesia. The **royal cemetery** where he is buried is at Astana on the grounds of the Gunung Jati Mosque, seven kilometres out of town. Four kilometres from town is the **Sunya Ragi**

pleasure palace built of rocks, tunnels, caves and secret chambers.
In the city are the *kratons*, or palaces of the sultans of Kasepuhan and Kanoman. Though sadly run down, they have museums that display armaments, paintings, calligraphy and other court treasures. The royal carriages are interesting, especially the one in the form of a winged elephant. The Cirebon rock-and-cloud design appears in many places.
Across the square from the palace is the **Mesjid Agung**, or Grand Mosque, made entirely of wood. In the colourful port are the warehouses from the Dutch East Indies days.
Cirebon is famous for its batik, often in blue and maroon with a cloud motif. Also popular is the brown-and-white lion motif. In the nearby village of **Trusmi** there is a flourishing batik industry in the small home workshops.
Cirebon Hotels: The Omega (★★★ 64 rooms. Jl. Tuparev 20, Tel. 3072), the Patra Jasa (★★★ 55 rooms. Jl. Tuparev 11, Tel. 3792) and the Grand (★★ 66 rooms. Jl. Siliwangi 9, Tel. 2014). All these hotels have restaurants and you can also try Chinese food at Maxim's, Jl. Bahagia 3.
A trip to Cirebon will be more interesting if you read *Cerbon*, published by Sinar Harapan and Mitrabudaya in Jakarta.

The Thousand Islands

. Although the only real swimming in Jakarta is in swimming pools, you can head off from this coastal city and in a few hours be past the polluted waters into tropical sea with beautiful beaches, sunning, snorkelling and diving.
The area off the coast of Jakarta is known as the Thousand Islands, or Pulau Seribu. Of the hundreds (thousand is an exaggeration) of islands, only a few are inhabited.
One, **Pulau Putri,** is especially popular with Jakarta residents and overseas tours. The island is four hours by boat, or a 25-minute flight by small plane from Kemayoran Airport in Jakarta to Pulau Panjang (Long island), which is nothing but an airstrip. From there you transfer to a simple ferry boat and take a 30-minute crossing to Pulau Putri.
On the island there are simple cottages with electricity at night, Western plumbing and an open beachside restaurant. A bathing suit and beach dress are all you need. You can rent waterskiing, scuba and snorkelling equipment, and there are little local sailboats that take you to nearby islands for shelling or snorkelling.
The whole trip can be arranged by making reservations through Putri Pulau Seribu Paradise, Jakarta Theatre Building, 9 Jl. Thamrin, Jakarta, Tel. 359333, Telex 441222 DARMA JKT. Price for 4 days is US$425 per person, including air transportation to the island, meals and accommodation.

Carita Beach

They also offer overnight packages to **Papa Theo Dive Camp,** which is more rustic but has breathtakingly beautiful diving and snorkelling close to shore. Also ask about the hydrofoil service. One word of caution: before embarking on your trip, make sure that your boat is equipped with a radio and lifejackets. Breakdowns do occur. If you want to go for just the day, inquire about their tours to **Pulau Perak** for Rps 49,000 per person, including transportation and lunch.

Samudra Beach

Another popular weekend escape for Jakarta residents is Samudra Beach, also known as Pelabuhan Ratu, on the south coast of Java, a 3½-hour (155 kms) drive over mountain terrain through Bogor and the Puncak pass. This is a beautiful area, with high waves and a black sand beach. Swimming can be treacherous and regularly claims lives. In the morning visit the village fish market, or hire a local fishing boat.

Samudra Hotels: Hotel Samudra Beach (★★★★ 106 rooms. Tel. 23, Telex 45724). This is a slightly rundown highrise hotel with a pool, tennis and mini-golf. It sits right on the beach, which can be treacherous, but has a large pool at beachside. A smaller hotel is the Pondok Dewata (Tel. 25) on a beach with safe swimming. The Bayu Armta (Tel. 31) has simple cliffside cottages and is well known for its very good seafood restaurant.

Anak Krakatau, a live volcano off Carita Beach

Carita Beach

Another beach resort popular on weekends with Jakarta residents is Carita Beach. It is 190 kilometres southwest of Jakarta, a difficult 4½-hour drive. The Carita Krakatau Beach Hotel (★★) offers seaside cottages, but the beach and peaceful water are heavenly. Book through the Menteng Hotel, Jl. Gondangdia Lama 28, Jakarta, Tel. 325208.

The Menteng Hotel office can also make arrangements for your visit to the **Krakatau** and **Ujung Kulon Nature Reserves.** Krakatau is the famous volcano that exploded in 1883, losing half its area and sending tidal waves across the Indian Ocean to the shores of Africa, taking 30,000 lives. Now one can see the cone of Krakatau and other islands, including Anak Krakatau.

From Carita Beach you can arrange to go by boat to Krakatau, 40 kilometres away. Boats rent for about Rps 200,000 for the ten-hour round trip, and you should bring along all the water, food and drinks you will need for the day.

Ujung Kulon is a wildlife reserve on the western tip of West Java. Its 51,000 hectares are covered with dense forest, and it is the home of the last surviving one-horned rhinoceros. There are also wild ox, deer, wild bear, panthers, crocodiles, snakes and birds. Accommodation is rustic, and all food and water should be taken in. There are beautiful untouched beaches and wonderful coral formations. The trip, however, is only for the very adventurous nature lover.

To reach the reserve, drive to the village of Labuhan (3-5 hours from Jakarta) and charter a local fishing boat or government-owned guard boat for the five to nine-hour trip by sea to the peninsula. Park headquarters are at Tamanjaya. Before you go, get an entry permit from the Directorate of Nature Conservation and Wildlife Management (Direktorat Perlindungan dan Pengawetan Alam, Jl. Juanda 9, Bogor, West Java) and obtain a copy of the brochure *Indonesia: Ujung Kulon National Park* from the Directorate-General of Tourism of Indonesia, Jl. Kramat Raya 81, P.O. Box 409, Jakarta. A visit to the reserve requires at least three to five days including transportation. To rent a boat from Labuhan for three days costs Rps 250,000-350,000 per person.

Central Java

Central Java is tops on most tourists' lists. The most popular itinerary is to fly to the city of Yogyakarta and spend two or three nights soaking up the area's rich culture, artistry and history before flying east to Bali or returning to Jakarta. Tourism is quite well developed here, and English is frequently spoken.

For those with more time and a greater sense of adventure, the drive from Jakarta to Yogyakarta goes through rice fields, past volcanoes and allows you to stop at the north coastal ports (once the centres of Muslim kingdoms) and the beaches of the south coast, some of which are black and eerie. For details of the Jakarta—Yogyakarta—Surabaya train, see the *East Java* section, page 77.

Central Java has a long and rich history. The remains of Java Man (*pithecanthropus erectus*) were found near Solo and are among the earliest known hominid fossils ever found.

In the 7th to 10th centuries powerful Central Javanese dynasties arose, building the fantastic Buddhist Borobudur monument and the Hindu Prambanan temple complex, which rate among the world's most important religious monuments.

In the 16th and 17th centuries Central Java was the seat of the Mataram empire, which was marked by wars, conquests and intrigue. In 1775 the Dutch, who were by then firmly in control of Java while at the same time allowing local regents to rule, divided the empire in two. This split created the court of Mangkunegoro in Yogyakarta and the court of Hamengkubuwono in nearby Solo. These palaces became havens of cultural refinement, with court dance, *gamelan* music and finely crafted batik appreciated by all. In 1946 Yogyakarta temporarily became the capital of the newly-declared Republic of Indonesia while the Dutch still claimed control of the country from their capital in Jakarta. With the recognition of independence, the capital of the new nation moved to Jakarta.

Yogyakarta

Yogyakarta is a key tourist spot because of its pleasant hotels, interesting cultural sights and beautiful scenery. It is located at the foot of the active volcano Mount Merapi in a fertile plain that was once the seat of the mighty Mataram empire. It is now the home of Gajah Mada University, named after the prime minister of the Majapahit Kingdom.

Getting Around

From Jakarta and Bali there are daily flights to Yogyakarta on Garuda Airlines. Many of the hotels have cars at the attractive little airport to meet their guests, or you can hire a taxi for the short ride into town.

When sightseeing in Yogyakarta, rent a *becak* pedicab for about Rps 1,500 for two hours. This is a unique way to see the city as you slowly bump along the back streets, stopping to admire whatever catches your fancy.

Taxis are available through your hotel at Rps 3,500 per hour without airconditioning, 4,200 per hour with. The driver can take you to the major sights in town, drive you to the Borobudur and Prambanan temples and take you to an evening cultural performance. He'll obligingly wait to bring you home at the end of the evening.

Sights in Yogyakarta

The *kraton*, or palace, at the southern end of the *alun alun* (traditional town square, always with an enormous *waringin* tree in the middle) is the key sight. It is treasured as the archetype of classical Javanese architecture with its wide, swept courtyards and *pendopo* (open-sided pavilion) with carved pillars. The palace has English-speaking guides who will show you the traditional *gamelan* orchestra, a Western-style stained glass music pavilion and carved palanquins used for royal weddings. The family retainers who stroll through the courtyards wear traditional batik with ceremonial daggers (*kris*) stuck in their waistbands. The royal family, still highly respected, continues to live here, and the classical court dances and ceremonies are still held here.

In the **kraton museum** you will see royal portraits by Raden Saleh, royal heirlooms and gifts from royal guests of the past. Though the whole palace has a slightly down-at-the-heels appearance, there is an unmistakable old-time refinement and grace about the place. Note that the *kraton* is open from 9am to 12.30pm every morning except Friday, when it closes at 11.30am. It's best to get up bright and early in Yogyakarta, as many of the public buildings of interest are closed in the afternoon. Save trips to the Borobudur, Prambanan and shopping for the afternoon.

At the **Sono Budoyo Museum** near the *kraton* on the northern side of

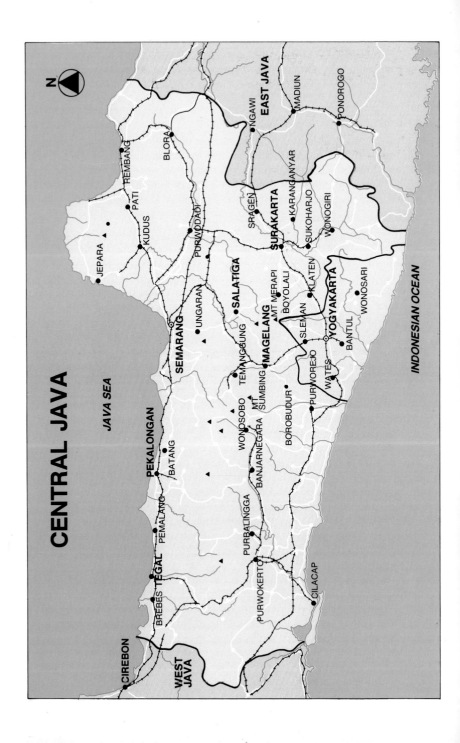

Men in traditional dress in the palace grounds, Yogyakarta

the city's main square you can see Buddha figures, *wayang* figures, a *gamelan*, *kris*, and textiles. Open 8am-1pm Tuesday and Thursday, 8-11am Friday and Sunday, Saturday 8am-noon. Closed Mondays.

The **Taman Sari**, or 'Water Castle', was built in 1758 by Sultan Hamengkubuwono I as a vast pleasure park. Today it is in ruins, but with its pools, arches and underground passageways it is fun to imagine its days of grandeur when royalty was here at play. In the Taman Sari area there are many little batik shops, one of which teaches a mini-course in batik to foreigners.

Sights Outside Yogyakarta

An absolute must is a visit to the **Borobudur** monument. Borobudur is the world-famous Buddhist sanctuary built around AD 800 by the Sailendra dynasty. It is an enormous mountain of grey andesite stone created in seven receding terraces which rise up to a great stupa 40 metres above the ground. Don't be daunted by the climb up its side as this, too, is a must. First climb up the steps to the first level and walk around the entire monument, taking in the stone reliefs along the processional path. Then climb up to the next level and repeat the tour around the monument. The reliefs show delightful scenes: romantic forays, storm-swept ships, cavorting monkeys and pious believers. Most important are the scenes from the life and teachings of Buddha. The niches along the way hold larger-thanlifesize Buddhas that look with tranquillity over the surrounding countryside. At the top is a circular terrace with bell-shaped stupas and a fabulous, inspirational view of the surrounding greenery and mountains. The monument is considered a world-class treasure, and has recently been restored through an international effort costing hundreds of thousands of dollars.

Late afternoon is the nicest time to visit the Borobudur, when the countryside is emerald green. If you visit at midday be sure to wear a hat to shield you from the sun. Have lunch at the restaurant run by the Ambarrukmo Hotel, which is a short drive away. Guidebooks are available at the site.

When visiting Borobudur make sure to stop at two smaller temples, known as *candi,* along the way. Three kilometres from the Borobudur is **Candi Mendut,** an intimate temple of piled-up stone set within a small field where sheep graze.

Climb up the short flight of steps and walk along the processional path around the temple, making sure you don't trip over the stone block that stands right in the middle of the path. Then enter the single chamber. Still, cool and quiet, the chamber envelops you as your eyes slowly make out the images of two bodhisattvas and a three-metre-tall Buddha whose tranquil beauty makes it one of the greatest Buddhist statues in the world. Don't miss this statue.

Candi Pawon, nearby, is another pleasing little temple surrounded by palms along the side of the road.

Seventeen kilometres east of Yogyakarta is the **Prambanan** temple. Because the Prambanan and the Borobudur are on opposite sides of Yogyakarta, you can visit them on separate days or see them on the same day.

The Prambanan is a Hindu temple complex built in the 9th century. Its name derives from the village where it is located, though it is known locally as the Loro Jonggran Temple, or Temple of the Slender Virgin.

Like the Borobudur, it is covered with stone bas-reliefs, here depicting tales from the Hindu epic, the *Ramayana.* In the main temple of Shiva, which rises to 130 feet, there are four chambers holding magnificent stone statues of Shiva, Shiva's consort Durga, Agastya (the sage who is said to have brought Hinduism from India to Indonesia) and Ganesha, the elephant god who is a favourite with students and is the overcomer of obstacles.

The Prambanan is a temple complex of eight shrines, the three main ones being dedicated to Shiva, Vishnu and Brahma. The Indonesian government is currently restoring the complex.

While you are visiting Prambanan, ask your driver to take you to other small temples nearby: **Candi Sewu, Candi Sari, Candi Kalasan** and **Candi Plaosan.** During the full moon in May to October, return to the

Prambanan at night for a performance of the *Ramayana* ballet (see section on Yogyakarta performing arts, page 72).

Other Sights out of Yogyakarta

If you have the time and inclination, there are other sights of interest in the area. Visit the village of **Kota Gede**, six kilometres southeast of Yogyakarta, a neat little town once the seat of the mighty Mataram empire. It is the centre of Yogyakarta silverwork, and there are several workshop showrooms where talented craftsmen create filigree jewellery, silver statues, bowls, tea services and bracelets.

A country village is the home of Pak Warno Waskito, a friendly, elderly man known for his carving of **masks** and wooden *wayang golek* puppets. Take the Bantul road south from Yogyakarta, turn right at the 7.6-kilometre marker and walk 300 metres.

Heading back on the road to Yogya, turn left at the 6.5-kilometre post and follow the road about one kilometre to the village of **Kasongan.** Here the whole village sets to work creating terracotta pots and well-designed animal figures. The designs are excellent, having been created some twenty years ago and copied ever since, and the prices are unbelievably low (Rps 3,000-15,000) for mythical beasts, elephants and lions. Watch them fire the sculptures in smoky bundles of straw.

Imogiri, twenty kilometres south of Yogya, is the site of the royal tombs. The famous Sultan Agung was buried here in 1645, and succeeding Mataram princes and royal families from Yogyakarta and Solo have been buried here since. To reach the tombs, climb 345 steps under shading boughs. The tombs are in courtyards, and entrance is only permitted on Monday and Friday. To enter you must wear traditional Javanese dress, which can be rented on the spot. Imogiri may be disappointing when the tombs are closed, although it is always a delightfully tranquil place.

Shopping in Yogyakarta

No one leaves Yogyakarta empty-handed, and even non-shoppers will enjoy shopping, because you can often see the craftsmen at work and you are always welcome to stop, talk and take pictures. For famous Yogyakarta silver visit Srimoeljo's Silver at Jl. Menteri Supeno UH XII/1a, Tel. 88042. In the silver village of Kota Gede you'll see craftsmen at work at Tom's Silver and MD Silver.

To see *wayang puppets* carved out of buffalo hide, created into fascinating figures with lacy designs painted in gold and other colours, visit the demonstration at Moeljosoehardjo's, Jl. Taman Sari 37B or at Swastigita. The puppets all have names, from the fat-bellied clown Semar to the refined Krishna and Sinta, whose long noses and heads look downwards in a pose of refinement. The leaf-shaped *kayon* puppet represents the tree of life and is used to mark scene changes during the puppet show. Prices run from Rps 10,000 to 100,000 depending on workmanship.

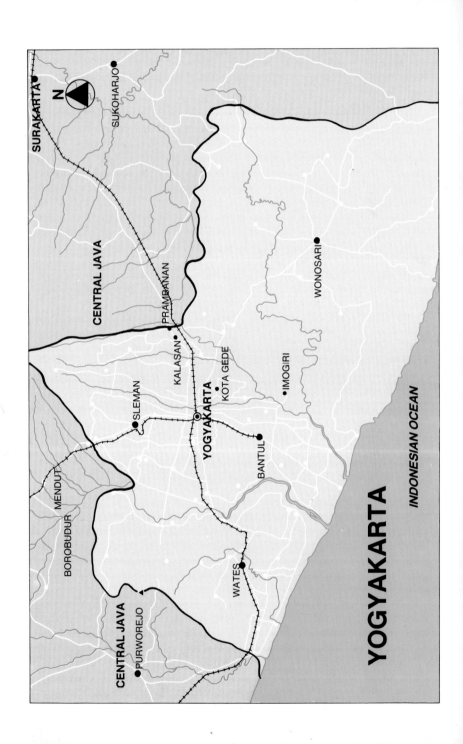

YOGYAKARTA

INDONESIAN OCEAN

Stone relief at Borobudur Temple

Yogyakarta is known for light-coloured, thick, sturdy, hand-tooled pocketbooks, sandals and other **leather** items. Check the quality of the stitching before you buy. Especially beautiful leather at Budi Group, Jl. Muju Muja 21.

As an arts centre Yogyakarta has a number of **art galleries.** Sapto Hudoyo (Jl. Solo, Kilometre 9, Megumo, Tel. 87443) is an elegant man with an elegant home, gallery and showroom. There are modern paintings by Sapto Hudoyo himself, and works by other local artists.

The studio-gallery of Affandi on Jalan Solo just out of town is also worth a visit. Although some of the works which made Affandi a sort of national hero in the art world are on permanent display, there are other works for sale by Affandi, his daughter Kartika and several young artists. To see young artists at work visit ASRI (the Academy of Fine Arts) in Gampingan.

Batik is sold everywhere as sarongs, blouses, dresses, shirts, toys and wall hangings. Hunt around the shops in the Taman Sari area or visit Batik Garuda on Jalan Parangtritis 77B or Winotosastra on Jalan Tirtodipuran, Tel. 2218. If you would like to know more about the methods of making batik by *cap* (stamp) or *tulis* (hand-drawn) methods, visit the permanent displays at the Balai Penelitian Batik dan Kerajinan (Batik Handicraft Research Centre) on Jalan Kusumanegara. For batik paintings visit Amri

Yahya's gallery and workshop in the western part of the city at Jalan Gampingan 67 off Jalan Wates.

Pasars, the market **bazaars** filled with everything under the sun, are a highlight of Yogyakarta. At the Pasar Beringharjo, the main market at the end of Jalan Malioboro (Yogya's main street) there is an enormous selection of batik in three-metre lengths. Everything else is here too, from herbs and spices to brass pots. Hang on to your purse.

At Pasar Ngasem, a quieter *pasar*, you'll find charcoal braziers, water jugs and brightly coloured money boxes in animal forms made of terracotta. The Bird Market near the Water Castle is another interesting stop.

Performing Arts in Yogyakarta

At the centre of Central Javanese court culture, Yogyakarta is a good place to see traditional, refined **dances** accompanied by large *gamelan* orchestras. The **Ramayana Ballet,** based on the Indian epic, is performed at the outdoor stage of the Prambanan temple from June through October. With a cast of hundreds and two *gamelan* orchestras providing the music, shows are held from 7 to 9pm on four consecutive nights during the full moon of each month. The setting is lovely and, while not everyone in the cast is a fine dancer, the main dancers give excellent performances of classical Javanese dance. Tickets available through your travel agent in Yogyakarta or at the performance.

Classical Javanese dance is performed Wednesday and Friday from 8 to 10pm at Pujukusuman near Pojok Beteng, southeast of the *kraton* near Jalan Katamso. The Ambarrukmo Hotel has a cultural show nightly except Monday on the seventh floor.

Nightly performances of *wayang wong*, a play starring classical characters and accompanied by *gamelan*, is held at the People's Park (Taman Hiburan Rakyat). They say Saturday night can be lively, but on the night we went the cast was dismal and there were only four people in the audience.

Dance rehearsals are good to visit to help you appreciate the difficulty of this slow and refined dance style, and to see the intensity of the young people who are keeping alive this age-old Javanese tradition. Catch a rehearsal at ASTI (the Indonesian Academy of Dance) or at the studio of Bagong Kusudiarjo in the afternoons at Jalan Singosaren 9, near Jalan Wates. Bagong Kusudiarjo is also a well-known painter. On Sunday mornings from 10am to 1pm there are classical court dance practices at the *kraton*. A good time to visit.

Wayang, the classical shadow puppet play, is performed for the residents of Yogya on the second Saturday night of each month at the Sasono Hinggil Dwi Abad on the town square, or *alun alun*. The performance lasts all night and you are able to come and go as you please.

There is a shortened version of *wayang*, just to give you an idea of how it is performed, at the Yayasan Kesenian Agastya at Gedong Kiwa II/221 just off Jalan Bahl every day from 3 to 5pm. A *wayang kulit* performance for tourists is held at the Yayasan Ambar Budaya opposite the Hotel Ambarrukmo every Monday, Wednesday and Saturday from 9.30 to 10.30pm, and a *wayang golek* (wooden puppet) show for tourists at Nitour, Jalan Dahlan 71 every day from 10am to noon.

Gamelan, the classical orchestra which accompanies all performances, is played at the palace from 10am to noon on Mondays and Wednesdays. Inquire at your hotel or guest house to confirm the above times and to find out about special local performances held in connection with local holidays.

Hotels in Yogya

The **Ambarrukmo Palace** (★★★★ 240 rooms on Jl. Adisucipto, Tel. 88488, Telex 12511) is an international-style hotel with pool, several restaurants and all facilities. The hotel is on the site of a former palace, and if you are lucky you may catch a traditional Javanese wedding in the Javanese *pendopo* hall of the former palace.

Everyone's favourite place is the **Puri Artha Hotel,** a highly recommended small hotel (★★★ Jl. Cendrawasih 9, Tel. 5934, Telex 25147). It's set in a garden with a small pool. The standard rooms (all airconditioned) are just fine, but especially nice are the top-of-the-line rooms with carved Balinese doors and enormous carved Chinese canopy beds. Complimentary tea and fried bananas await you on the veranda outside your room when you come home from sightseeing. The veranda restaurant, lighted by romantic gas lamps, is good and open to the public.

More centrally located is the **Mutiara Hotel** on Jl. Malioboro 18, Tel. 45301. Airconditioned with a nice restaurant. There are also several good guest houses on Jalan Prawirotaman. Try the **Wisma Gajah** at 2A (Tel. 2479) and **Sumaryo Guest House** at 18A (Tel. 2852). The host is very helpful at the homestay of **Sri Puger,** Jl. Haryono (Jl. Pugeran) 9, Yogya, Tel. 5545. The Rps 10,000 charge includes breakfast.

Restaurants in Yogya

The **Puri Artha** has a very pleasant garden restaurant and the **Ambarrukmo Hotel** has a variety of coffee shops and formal restaurants serving European and Indonesian dishes. The best fried chicken is at **Nyonya Suharti MBok Berek** on Jalan Solo, one kilometre east of the Ambarrukmo. Try Chinese food at **Sintawang,** Jl. Magelang, Tel. 2901. *Nasi gudeg,* the traditional chicken dish cooked for hours in a clay pot, is best at **Andrawina Loka Gudeg Bu Tjitro** on Jalan Adisucipto.

Solo

Solo, also known as Sala and Surakarta, is a good place to visit for a day or two in connection with your trip to Yogyakarta. There is a good small airport in Solo if you are coming from Jakarta direct. To get to Solo from

Yogya, hire a car and driver at your hotel to drive you the one-hour ride. Stop at the Prambanan temple between the two cities.

Solo is a pleasant city located in a lush area surrounded by rice fields. In the distance on a clear day you'll see her surrounding volcanoes: Mt Lawu, Mt Merapi and Mt Merbabu. To get around the best bet is to walk or to hail a *becak*. Why not rent a horse and carriage for an hour or two? More conventional travel is available in taxis rented by the hour at your hotel.

Sightseeing in Solo

Like Yogya, Solo is known for its refined court culture, and a visit to one or both of the palaces is a must. The **Kraton Solo,** the Sunan's Palace, is the larger of the two. It is an enormous walled area several city blocks wide with courtyards, gardens, buildings and open platforms. Located south of the town square, it is open from 9am to noon every morning. At the palace museum there are Javanese heirlooms and antiques. Not far from this palace is a *wayang beber* artist who makes scrolls used in story-telling. His workshop is at Jalan Baluwerti 80. At Jalan Gambuhan 30 there is a workshop where *gamelan* instruments are made.

The palace of the second ruling house in Solo is the **Mangkunegaran Palace.** It too is a series of walled courtyards, gardens and pavilions, one of which houses a very fine little museum of royal treasures such as *kris*, dance jewellery, wooden *topeng* masks and bronzes from the Hindu-Buddhist period. If you are lucky, your tour guide may gain permission to take you through the private family rooms.

The **Solo Museum** on Jalan Slamet Riyadi is open from 9am to noon and has a small collection of artefacts. The **Grand Mosque** is at the west side of the town square.

There is a **Chinese temple** to visit right across the street from the **Pasar Besar** (Big Market). This market holds a vast array of fruits, vegetables and household items. There are some handsome old Dutch colonial buildings on Jalan Slamet Riyadi, Jalan Sudirman and Jalan Urip Sumohardjo which now house banks, offices, the mayor's residence, etc.

In the evening, take a *becak* over to the **Sriwedari Gardens** for a performance of the famous *wayang wong* troupe, which performs nightly except Sunday. Although the performance is in Javanese, you'll still enjoy the sparkling proscenium stage, the glittering costumes, first-class makeup and dramatic qualities which transcend language. There are pompous warriors, slapstick buffoons and refined princesses.

Dance practices are open to spectators' eyes at the **Sasono Mulyo,** the music and dance academy of the *kraton* located within the palace walls to the west of the main gate. Practices are held on Tuesday and Friday from 1 to 3pm and 6-8pm. *Gamelan* practices are on Mondays (7-9pm), Wednesdays (3-6pm), Thursdays (1-3pm) and Saturdays (2-4pm).

At the Mangkunegaran Palace you are welcome to visit *gamelan* practices on Saturdays from 10am to noon and dance practices on Wednesdays from 10am to noon.

Sights Outside Solo

Stop at the Surakarta Tourist Office on Jalan Slamet Riyadi to the left of the entrance to Sriwedari Gardens. Go with a car and driver to **Sangiran, 15** kilometres north, an archaeological excavation site with a mini-museum of prehistoric fossils. This area along the Solo River has yielded major finds such as the remains of Java Man, found in 1891. **Tawangmangu** is a mountain resort about one hour from Solo on the slopes of Mount Lawu. **Candi Sukuh** is a pyramid-shaped temple 21 kilometres east of Solo, 900 metres up Mount Lawu. It is a 14th century Hindu temple known for the bas-reliefs in *wayang* style and for its erotic sculpture. Beautiful mountain scenery along the way.

Shopping in Solo

Pasar Klewer is the batik textile market where you'll find batik ($3-$50), striped *lurik* in subtle colours ($3), gaudy costume jewellery for traditional dance performances ($5-$10) and bright sashes ($1.50). Bargain! Pasar Trewindu on Jalan Diponegoro is an antique and junk bazaar where you can bargain for Dutch crockery, coal-heated irons, Buddha heads and the like. Get top quality batik at Danar Hadi (caftans $10-$25; dresses $5-$25).

East Java

One of Java's three provinces, East Java is a diverse and beautiful area. Much like neighbouring Bali and Central Java, it has terraced rice fields, banana and papaya trees and towering volcanoes. It is, however, less well travelled, and so the scenic views can be enjoyed in greater tranquillity.

On the north is the flat coastal plain with natural harbours that historically saw traders from the Middle East, India and China. Even today the main port of Surabaya is Indonesia's second largest city, and a bustling port of three million people. To the west and along the south are volcanoes and landscapes of great natural beauty. In the countryside are well-tended villages and intimate temples. On the eastern coast is a vast wild animal reserve. The island of Madura, administratively part of East Java, is only a 20-minute ride from Surabaya.

History

As the power of Central Java declined around the 10th century, other powerful kingdoms arose in East Java. Between 1055 and 1222 the kingdom of Kediri prospered and expanded. During the reign of King Erlangga, both East Java and Bali enjoyed a lucrative trade with surrounding islands, and their arts flourished. Parts of the Indian *Mahabharata* epic were translated and interpreted to conform to the East Javanese outlook and

Misty morning scene from the train to Bandung

philosophy, and it was from this era that East Java gained much of its temple art.

In 1222 the Singasari dynasty came into power, and during this period several of the main temples were built, mainly to honour the kings of the dynasty. In 1292 East Java's Majapahit empire came to the fore, dominating the entire archipelago, the Malay peninsula and part of the Philippines. Profitable trade relations with China and other neighbouring countries were established. At the end of the 16th century the Mataram empire established itself. Unfortunately there is not much left to mark East Java's glorious past apart from the small temples in the countryside.

During the Dutch colonial period Surabaya was an important trading port, as it still is today. When Indonesia declared its independence in 1945 the Dutch and their British allies refused to accept that a new nation had been born. British troops landed in Surabaya and a full-fledged battle began, with many bombings and deaths.

Arriving in East Java

The main port of entry into East Java is Surabaya, which has flights to Jakarta, Yogyakarta and Bali on a daily basis. For the adventurous traveller who loves trains, there is an 18-hour night train from Jakarta to Surabaya via Yogyakarta. Known as the *Bima*, the train leaves Jakarta at 4.30pm daily. First class has two berths per cabin; second class has three. Not luxurious, but adequate. Buy bottled drinks on the train as the water is not potable. Indonesian food is available in the very plain dining car. Buy your tickets in Jakarta at Carnation Travel, Jl. Menteng Raya 24.

To drive the 800 kilometres from Jakarta to Surabaya takes two full days. The ferry from Java to Bali leaves Banyuwangi in East Java several times a day and goes to Gilimanuk in western Bali. A good road connects Gilimanuk with Denpasar in south Bali.

Getting Around

East Java is best seen in a leisurely way by private car with a driver. Each of the hotels in Surabaya has a travel agent who can arrange a car and driver for you to tour the sites of East Java and Madura. Especially recommended is Lily at the Pacto office Jl. Pemuda 78 (Tel. 472706). She speaks good English and is willing to take the time to discuss travel plans in detail.

A Suggested Itinerary

Day 1 Tour Surabaya.

Day 2 Take a day trip to Madura to see a bull race (only on weekends) and tour the island. Return to Surabaya.

Day 3 Transfer to the mountain resort of Tretes, about one hour outside Surabaya. At midnight leave for an all-night and early morning trip to see the memorable sunrise at Mount Bromo.

Day 4 Return to Tretes from Mount Bromo and spend a day relaxing, touring small local temples and walking or horseback riding in the area. See a cultural performance at Pandaan in season.

Day 5 Travel by car south to see Candi Kidal and Candi Jawi. Spend the night at Malang or the mountain towns of Batu or Selecta.

Day 6 Tour Candi Panataran and return to Surabaya.

When arranging your tour, make sure that all arrangements are agreed upon in advance to cover the driver's meals, lodging and payment.

Surabaya

Surabaya's *raison d'etre* is business and trade. Because of its commercial importance it is perhaps less interesting for the tourist than other parts of Indonesia. A tour of Surabaya can be consolidated into a few hours on either end of a tour of the rest of East Java.

Sights

The port, called Tanjung Perak, is filled with ocean-going cargo ships and traditional schooners for inter-island trade. The **Surabaya Zoo** on Jalan Raya Diponegoro has an impressive animal collection, a sea aquarium and a nocturama housing endangered species such as the slow loris. Afterwards have a pastry at Delby, a cake shop across from the zoo.

Jane's House (Jl. Dinoyo 100, Tel. 67722) used to take paying guests, but no more. Tourists are still welcome to tour the fantastic collection of antique furniture, heavily carved Chinese beds, chests and hanging lamps, all for sale—at a high price.

The **Tugu Pahlawan** is a monument honouring Indonesian freedom fighters. The **Joko Dolog Statue** represents the 13th century King Kartenegara in his Buddhist incarnation.

Shopping

There are beautiful antiques, especially furniture, at the shop of Frans Logantara, Jl. Embong Wungu 30, Tel. 44948. Frans and his wife Tje Tje are knowledgeable and trustworthy. Pinguin (Jl. Suryani 45) has a good selection of European, Chinese and Indonesian antiques. Local crafts at Toko Bali on Jalan Basuki Rachmat. Batik clothes at Batik Keris (Jl. Tanungan 1) and Danar Hadi (Jl. Basuki Rachmat). Soesparhadi on Jalan Sumatra sells distinctive maroon and navy Madura batik and woodcarvings made behind her home.

On the road between Surabaya and Malang in Pokasari is Bob's Barang Lama, an excellent antique shop with good furniture selections. Coming from Surabaya, the shop is located just before the Botanical Garden. Closed Tuesday. Bob can arrange for shipment of purchases.

Evening Entertainment

Ask at your hotel where you can see a performance of traditional *kuda kepang,* a trance dance where dancers ride around on narrow hobby horses and other performers do bizarre things like munch electric lightbulbs and climb ladders made of sword blades.

During the dry season, May to September, make the hour-long trip out of Surabaya to see the classical Javanese dance performances held in the evenings at Candra Wilwatikta, the temple at Pandaan.

Restaurants in Surabaya

Fancy, expensive and delicious is Hugo's Restaurant in the Hyatt Hotel. The best Chinese restaurant, and also the most expensive, is at the Garden Hotel (Jl. Pemuda 21, Tel. 470000). Chez Rose is, like Jane's House, a Surabaya institution. Since Dutch days it has changed little. There's a Japanese restaurant at the Mirama Hotel (Jl. Raya Darmo 69-78, Tel. 69501). The Quai Wah is a rooftop restaurant popular with local people who like the steamboat dinner. Book a table in advance. The Bon Cafe is an old Dutch house with shades of the past. The Aloha Restaurant is a top Chinese restaurant, about 25 minutes out of town. Noisy atmosphere but good food.

Hotels in Surabaya

Surabaya's ritziest hotel is the Hyatt Bumi (★★★★) which is a first-class new hotel with a Clark Hatch physical fitness centre at Jl. Basuki Rachmat, Tel. 470875, Telex 31391. Also popular are the Simpang (★★★★ 128 rooms,

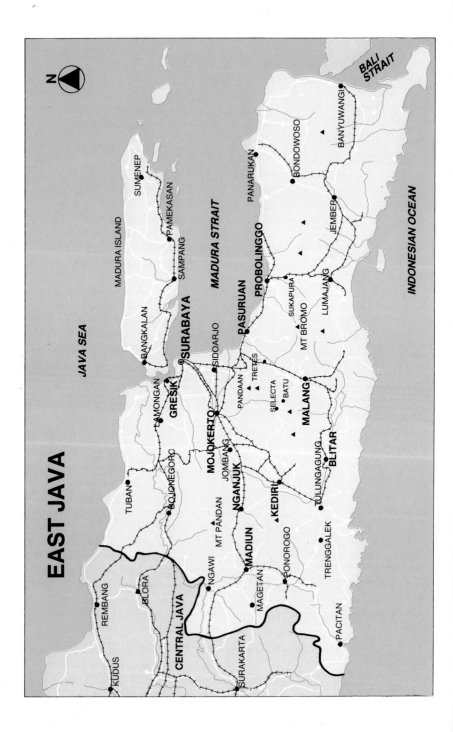

Tenggarese rider at Mount Bromo

Jl. Pemuda 1-3, Tel. 42150, Telex 31607), the Elmi (★★★ 74 rooms, Jl. Panglima Sudirman 42, Tel. 471570, Telex 31431) and the Garden (★★★ 100 rooms, Jl. Pemuda 21, Tel. 470000, Telex 31428).

Other Places to Know

The Indonesian Government Immigration Office is at Jalan Keputih 49A. There are several foreign consulates in Surabaya. The American Consulate can send you in the right direction if you have a problem. They are at 33 Jl. Dr Sutomo, Tel. 69287. The East Java Tourist Office is at Jl. Yos. Sudarso 3.

Madura

Accommodation, such as in the Trunojoyo Hotel in Pamekasan, is very simple. Therefore it is best to make a day trip to Madura out of Surabaya. Make arrangements through Pacto travel agency in the Mirama Hotel.

Madura is a flat and dry island, spotted with farms raising cattle, poultry and goats. The people of the island are devoutly Muslim and for this reason it is best not to dress immodestly (including wearing bathing suits) there. The Madurese are well known for their hot tempers, so stay away from altercations.

Madura is renowned for its bull races, held at island villages during the dry season (April to October). The climax of the season is the **Kerapan**

Besar, a colourful race and fair held at the town square in the island's capital of Pamekasan. Be careful when attending a bull race as the crowds of excited spectators swerve to get out of the way of the teams of brightly decorated, charging bulls.

Your day trip to Madura will begin with the 20-minute ferry crossing from Surabaya to Madura—very colourful and fascinating to watch the ferry fill to bursting with cars and goods of every description. Most people drive to Pamekasan and also stop at **Sumenep,** an interesting town with a *kraton* (palace) museum. Make sure you get there in the morning as things close early.

Tretes

A perfect antidote to Surabaya's bustle and congestion is Tretes, a hill town about one hour away which is known for its lovely, well-kept houses, flower gardens and cool mountain air. Tretes is a good base for a trip to see the sunrise over Mount Bromo.

In Tretes there are private bungalows and **hotels.** The Tanjung Plaza (★ ★ Jl. Wilis 7, Tel. 81102) is clean, attractive and newly rebuilt. Its rooms overlook a garden, and the dining room has a splendid view of the valley and volcanoes. Another hotel is the Natour Bath (★★★ 50 rooms, Jl. Pasanggrahan, Tel. 81161).

When in Tretes, walk to scenic waterfalls, swim in the hotel pool or take pony rides through the countryside.

Mount Bromo

Mount Bromo is famous for the dramatic sunrises seen from its peak. It takes quite a bit of effort to be there at sunrise, but the adventurous path has been well beaten by lots of travellers before you.

Have a late supper at your hotel in Tretes and, with your car and driver, depart around 11pm for the three-hour ride to Ngadisari. In the dark of night you will gather with a group of other adventurers, each mounting a scrawny little horse led by a sturdy Tenggarese guide. Wrapped in a blanket, sweater or light jacket (it's very cool), you'll slowly ride through villages where residents are sound asleep. There is darkness all around you and you will not know, on crossing a bridge, whether you are crossing a rivulet or a ravine. It's a silent, mystical pilgrimage.

Midway, stop for coffee at the Bromo Hotel in Sukapura. Some travellers stay at the Bromo Hotel, which cuts down on the long ride from Tretes. Most, however, prefer Tretes to the rustic accommodation here. When you near the rim of the cone of the volcano, dismount to climb the final 250 steps to the precipice.

Just then the sun rises in a colourful dawn. As you sit on the narrow rim of the cone, you can look down into the centre of the volcano, far below. As you come down the side of Bromo in daylight you'll see the floor of the large crater which surrounds it, a bleak desert of pumice stone and ash. Soon the desolation of the crater changes to the richly cultivated highlands of the region where potatoes, carrots, cabbages, corn, tomatoes and onions are planted in every available spot.

At the end of your Bromo experience return for a rest in Tretes.

Malang and the Temples

East Java is known for its small, almost intimate, temples scattered over the landscape within little villages and in fields along the wayside.

The best base for visiting the temples is the town of **Malang,** said to be the prettiest town in Java. Malang is 90 miles south of Surabaya and is a cool, clean place set in the hills. Dutch colonial architecture is in evidence, a reminder of the coffee and tobacco plantations that they established in the area. Stop in to buy baskets, flowers and antiques at Malang's **Pasar Besar** (Big Market). For regional tourist information stop in at the Tourist Development Board at Jalan Basuki Rachmat 72-76.

Malang Hotels: Pelangi Hotel (★★ Jl. Merdeka Selatan 3, Tel. 2004). Splendid Inn (★ Jl. Majapahit 2-4, Tel. 23860). It is centrally located and quiet in an old Dutch colonial building. The YMCA at Jalan Basuki Rachmat 72-74 is simple but clean, Tel. 23605.

Malang Restaurants: Toko Oen at Jalan Jend. Basuki Rachmat near the new Sarinah shopping centre serves European food. Two good Chinese restaurants are Ruman Makan Gajah Mada at Jalan Pasar Besar, and the Taman Sari at Jalan A. Dahlen. Spicy Minang food at Minang Jaya on Jalan Basuki Rachmat 22 near the YMCA.

Batu and Selecta

When touring East Java's temples you may also wish to make your base at Batu or Selecta, two quiet hill resorts about 45 minutes from Malang. These towns offer colourful roadside fruit and vegetable stands, walking in the cool air and horseback riding. **Hotels** in Batu are: the Asida (Jl. Panglima Sudirman 99, Tel. 259), which has swimming and tennis, the Palem (Jl. Trunojoyo 26, Tel. 177) and the Batu (Jl. Hasanuddin 4, Tel. 234). In Selecta is the Hotel Selecta (Jl. Tulungrejo, Tel. 25). The Restaurant Kenangan is a Chinese place beside the market in Batu.

The Temples

And now for the main purpose of your visit to the area: the temples. They are small, intimate buildings compared with the imposing monuments at Borobudur and Prambanan in Central Java. They were built to honour the kings of the Singasari and Majapahit dynasties. The Singasari dynasty (1222-1292) began and ended with an assassination and was a time of violence, short-lived kings and social disorder. Nevertheless the kings, who were revered as gods, had small temples built to honour themselves.

Candi Jawi, only seven kilometres from Tretes and 40 kilometres north of Malang, is a Shivaite-Buddhist sanctuary which is dedicated to King Kartanegara, the last king of the Singasari dynasty. It was built on a terrace surrounded by pools. The mixture of religions (so common in East Java) is seen in the Buddhist *dagob* at the top and the Hindu *yoni* in the central room. The narrative friezes along the side have not been identified.

Candi Singasari is a Shivaite-Buddhist sanctuary also dedicated to King Kartanegara and built around 1300. It is ten kilometres north of Malang and is the only building left of a former temple complex. Make sure to see the 3.8-metre tall *raksasas* (demons) and the statue of the sage Agastya in the surrounding garden.

Candi Jago was built in 1269 and was dedicated to the fourth Singasari king. It is 16 kilometres southeast of Malang. The body and roof have collapsed but the building is noteworthy for its relief sculpture in *wayang* style. The figures appear in partial profile just like the *wayang* puppets.

Candi Panataran is particularly beautiful. Here you will see a series of temples built in the 13th and 14th centuries during the Singasari and Majapahit dynasties. Most of the temples in the complex only have their bases remaining, although the main *naga*, or snake temple, is well preserved with reliefs showing stories from the traditional *Ramayana* and *Mahabharata* legends. Although it is a long drive to reach the temple, it is worth the effort partly due to the lovely setting within rice fields surrounded by beautiful trees. Inside the *naga* temple is a figure of the god Krishna.

Candi Kidal is a 13th century Shivaite temple dedicated to King Anuschapati, the second Singasari king. It is about 20 kilometres southeast of Malang and is small, but appealing. The reliefs show Garuda, the mythical bird and the Indonesian national symbol, carrying the nectar of immortality. There are elaborate carved stone medallions with animistic designs and *kala* heads on the main body.

Bali

There's no question that the most famous destination in Indonesia is Bali. For a start, it's a terrific place for a vacation for singles, nearly-weds, newlyweds, second honeymooners and families of all shapes and sizes. At Sanur and Kuta beaches you can easily fill a week's holiday swimming, dancing, playing tennis, windsurfing, shopping and drinking tropical punches which blur the outlines of the palm trees.

But that can be said of lots of beach resorts in this world. What, then, gives Bali its legendary charm? The answer is that Bali's gods have richly endowed the island with breathtaking natural beauty, where colour, light and shape work together to constantly amaze the eye. To these gods the gentle people of Bali have built temples in nearly every rice paddy and cliffside perch, and to these gods they make joyful, vibrant offerings of dance, music and towers of flowers and fruits. Every day. Every single day.

Perhaps nowhere else are craftsmen so active and prolific—painting landscapes of emerald fields, sculpting stone demons to frighten away bad spirits and, for tourists, carving five-foot high wooden palm trees with an eye to detail that only one who has lived among lush foliage all his life could achieve.

There's nothing obscure about Bali's bounty. The beauties of nature, life and art are richly spread over the island's volcanic slopes, ready for all of us to marvel at and to enjoy.

How long should you stay in Bali? Five days at least, a week or more if you can, so that you'll have enough time to swim and play, but also to savour the richness, creativity and wonder that make up this island which is so often accurately labelled 'magical'.

History

Bali's history stretches back to prehistoric times. Because the architecture is built in soft stone which is susceptible to the ravages of time, there is little left to remind us of Bali's earliest history. One notable exception, however, is the 'Moon of Pejeng', an enormous bronze drum from the Bronze Age in Indonesia (about 500 BC) that can be seen on a high pavilion at the Penataran Sasih Temple in Pejeng. There are records of a Balinese kingdom of Pejeng-Bedulu ruled by a dynasty of twins for seven generations in about AD 900.

Java and Bali shared common historical periods. The king of East Java from AD 989 to 1007, King Darmawangsa, extended his power over Bali. Subsequently King Erlangga (1019-1049), who was a Balinese prince with an East Javanese mother, became king of Kediri in East Java. During this period Javanese culture spread to Bali, bringing along the Hindu and Indian aspects that were alive in Javanese culture at that time. The Hindu religion, which was later replaced by Islam in Java, came to Bali and today forms the core of the religion of 95 percent of the people. The Indian epic stories, the *Ramayana* and the *Mahabharata*, were also brought to Bali, and form the basis of the dances and *wayang kulit* puppet performances that you will see during your stay on the island.

In 1049 Bali regained its independence from East Java, but was again dominated by Java in the 13th and 14th centuries. In the mid-16th century the rajah of Gelgel unified Bali and conquered territories in Java as well as on the islands of Lombok and Sumbawa. This was Bali's golden age, and the period of its greatest power in the archipelago. After the decline of this rajah, Bali's power declined: the conquered lands were lost and internal disagreement tore apart the principalities of the island.

Europeans first came to Balinese shores in the 16th century. A Portuguese expedition was shipwrecked off the coast, and around 1597 the Dutch explorer Cornelius deHoutman made an expedition to Bali. Despite the powerful hold that the Dutch had on Java, Bali remained essentially free of outside influences, and was ruled by independent and autonomous kings who continued to wage war with one another.

In 1855 the first Dutch government officer set up his headquarters in north Bali, and in 1882 the Dutch officially took control of the area. Regional wars continued among rival kings in independent south and central Bali. In 1904 Dutch troops landed in Sanur in south Bali and the ruling families fought a fight to the death which devastated the local people. In 1908 the Balinese kingdoms of Mengwi and Bangli were also subjected to Dutch rule.

Despite gaining power in Bali, the Dutch colonial government tried to protect the island from outside influences and exploitation between 1918 and 1942. During this period some education on Western lines came to Bali, and there was an artistic and cultural revival which was inspired by visiting foreign artists such as Walter Spies and Rudolf Bonnet, musicologists Jaap Kunst and Colin McPhee and anthropologists Margaret Mead, Gregory Bateson and Jane Belo.

Bali participated in Indonesia's fight for independence, and the airport near Denpasar is named after Lt Col. I Gusti Ngurah Rai, whose troops were defeated by Dutch forces in 1946.

Today Bali is an integral part of the nation of Indonesia, and a leader in Indonesia's tourist business. Despite the growth in tourism, with almost half a million tourists annually, the industry has been controlled so that tourist hotels are located primarily in the southern peninsula, leaving the rest of the island essentially unchanged and uniquely Balinese. The 2.3 million people of Bali live and work mainly as rice farmers in some 1,500 villages spread over the beautiful landscape.

Hotels

In Bali there is accommodation to please all kinds of travellers. Part of your decision on where to stay will depend on the kind of hotel you are looking for, and on the ambience of the area. In general, tourist hotels are confined to a few areas on the southern peninsula. Four and five-star hotels offer all the usual luxuries. The rest are often Balinese style in decor, with carved doors, beautifully thatched roofs and carved stone door-frames. Most are bungalow style, set in little gardens with verandas at the front.

One area on the southern peninsula is **Nusa Dua,** a newly developed resort with luxury facilities. Its only disadvantage is that it is somewhat isolated from other tourist activities. The **Sanur Beach** area on the eastern side of the southern peninsula has three large hotels, the Bali Beach, the

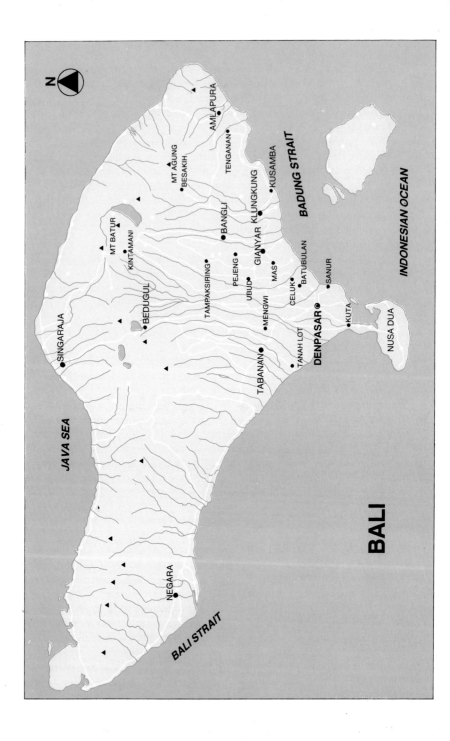

Rice terraces at Ubud, Bali

Sanur Beach and the Hyatt, as well as many small bungalow-style hotels all along the beach.

The area has many little curio shops and shacks selling bright locally-made clothing. There are lots of restaurants but the atmosphere is not as swinging as at Kuta Beach. The tide at Sanur is amazing, coming in high and calm for part of the day, then going far, far out for the rest of the day, leaving dramatic tidal pools which are good for building sand castles but terrible for swimming.

At **Kuta Beach** the atmosphere is very casual, with lots of budget travellers, many of them young and carefree. Kuta's cassette shops blast popular music into the street. Just up from Kuta is **Legian Beach** (pronounced 'Leg-ee-an', not like 'legion'), where the same atmosphere prevails. The only exceptions to the youthful, budget scene in Kuta and Legian are at Pertamina Cottages and the Oberoi, both posh and proper.

For those who want to feel closer to nature, closer to the daily life of Bali's craftsmen and people, a stay in **Ubud** is a must. This is a mountain town about one hour's drive from Kuta and Sanur. It is well known for the local and foreign artists who live in the area. There are beautiful walks in the rice fields and a feeling of relaxation and quiet. The accommodations are not elaborate, but they are pleasant, and there are a number of especially tasty little restaurants. Some visitors choose to spend their whole holiday at the beach, while others like to combine a few days at the beach with a couple of nights in Ubud.

In Ubud the early morning and end of the afternoon are best for walking around in the splendid local scenery. At midday it can be very hot, and you'll miss the swimming pools and ocean refreshment found at the beach resorts.

All prices listed below are for double rooms, excluding the 21 percent service and tax.

Sanur Hotels

On Sanur Beach there are two hotels which top the market in price and facilities. The **Bali Hyatt** (★★★★ $72-$87, Tel. 8271, Telex 35127) stands at one end of the beach and is a splendid integration of luxury chain hotel and Balinese atmosphere. The front lobby has the typical Balinese thatched roof, with traditional woodcarving on the lobby chairs. Little floral towers of frangipani, hibiscus and palm decorate the tables. Terracotta mythical figures spout fountains of water into the freeform pool. Non-resident guests can stop by for a poolside lunch or drink in the sunken pool bar. All rooms are in low-rise buildings, and there is a lively disco at night. The ground floor shopping arcade offers a comprehensive representation of all there is to buy in Bali. The Hyatt always looks full and active, especially with tour groups from around the world. On the beach there are facilities for sailing, waterskiing and windsurfing.

The **Bali Beach Inter-Continental** (★★★★ $72-$82, Tel. 5811, Telex 35129) is located at the other end of Sanur Beach. With 605 rooms, it is the only building in Bali which stands out above the palm trees. It was built in 1965 and its atmosphere is less Balinese than the Hyatt. It has several swimming pools and accommodations in the tower section of the main hotel as well as in the pleasant garden bungalows, all alongside the beach. There's a doctor's office in the hotel which is open to the public, mini-golf, shopping arcade, drugstore, golf course and supper club serving up Western food and international entertainment. As with all the big hotels in Bali, there is also a Balinese cultural show and dinner which is open to the public.

The **Sanur Beach Hotel** (★★★★ $72-$78, Tel. 8011, Telex 35135) also offers the facilities of a big hotel.

In addition to these international-style hotels, there are many bungalow colonies up and down the beach, all of which are located on the beach under waving palms. Most offer swimming pools and restaurants. They are all quite pleasant and offer accommodation in the $35 to $60 range.

A real favourite with repeat travellers to Bali is the **Tanjung Sari,** the oldest bungalow colony and, for my money, the best. While similar to the other bungalow hotels, its atmosphere is special and its prices are higher. The Tanjung Sari gives you the feeling that you are at your own little private club, or at your own charming beach house with a discreet staff. An appealing raised bar with carved demon chairs overlooks the beach and waving Balinese flags. There's a tiny pool with handcrafted blue and white tiles and Balinese sculpture. In the evening in the garden restaurant the sound of a bamboo *angklung* and a flute enhances the lush sense of romance. Ask for one of the airconditioned two-storey bungalows which have a cot and bath downstairs and, upstairs, a canopied bed in a tree-house environment. There are also one-storey family rooms that sleep four people comfortably. At the Tanjung Sari (★★ Tel. 8441, Telex 35157) bungalows run $80-$115.

Another popular Sanur hotel is **La Taverna** (★★ $55-$75, Tel. 8497, Telex 35163), which also has charming Balinese-style rooms decorated with Balinese arts and crafts. There is a small pool right next to its open-sided restaurant. Good Italian and Indonesian food there:

Santrian Beach Cottages (★★ $40, Tel. 8181, Telex 35169) is another bungalow-style hotel on the beach, with pool, restaurant and airconditioning.

For the really big splurge, consider renting one of the private villas in the **Batu Jimbar** complex. These are splendid Balinese-style, open villas decorated with magnificent rattan furniture, art and antiques. Each house is set in a garden along the beach and there is a pool and tennis court for complex residents. Each house comes with its own staff of servants. When the private owners are gone (they live all over the world) you can rent these memorable places for $150-$350 per day. Make arrangements through Tisnawati Hamid, Batujimbar Bungalows, c/o Hotel Tanjung Sari, P.O. Box 25, Denpasar, Tel. 8230, Telex 35157.

Nusa Dua

In newly-developed Nusa Dua is the **Nusa Dua Beach Hotel** (P.O. Box 1028, Denpasar, Tel. 71210, Telex 35206). It is a fancy resort with full sports facilities and Balinese decor. Check to see if Garuda is still offering its excellent package deals to the Nusa Dua. Prices run only slightly higher than airfare alone!

Keep your eyes open for the new **Club Med** resort (P.O. Box 1025, Tel. 71520, Telex 35216, 350 rooms).

Kuta Beach

On the Kuta Beach side of the tourist peninsula of south Bali are two luxury hotels which are separate from the youthful, swinging environment of the area. **Pertamina Cottages** (★★★★★ $88, Tel. 51061, Telex 35131) is a lovely international-style hotel set in a garden setting. The rooms are large and well suited to families, as there is a sliding screen between the bedroom and living/sleeping area in each unit. There is a large swimming pool, private beach (empty of the hawkers that pester you elsewhere), coffee shop and restaurants. Grounds are well manicured.

Up the beach at Legian is the luxurious **Bali Oberoi Beach Hotel** (Tel. 51061, Telex 35125). Ambassadors and the likes of Henry Kissinger stay here, and it is easy to see why. The hotel is very quiet and isolated. Though a mere 20 minutes from the airport, it can only be reached by taxi or hotel bus. There are double rooms ($80) which are pleasant enough, but the best bet, if you can afford it, are the glamorous villas ($150). Each villa is enclosed in its own walled courtyard, with bathrooms private yet out of doors, raised breakfast areas and Balinese-style canopy beds decorated with Balinese arts. There is a beach, pool and amphitheatre. If you don't stay there, it's still worth a visit just to see all the charming details in the decor.

In the Kuta area there is one inexpensive hotel which is a real charmer. It is **Poppie's Cottages** ($23; $5 extra with kitchen facilities. P.O. Box 378, Denpasar, Tel. 51059, 51419). Located off a little lane about five minutes' walk to the beach, it has pristine white Balinese-style bungalows in a lovely, neat little garden. Rooms are attractive and freshly decorated with batik bedspreads. Only drawback is that there is no pool. Located right across the lane from the ever-popular Poppie's Restaurant.

Other hotels in the Kuta area with swimming pools and Balinese-style bungalows on the beach are **Fourteen Roses** (Tel. 51156, 51835) and **Kartika Plaza Beach Hotel** ($36-$44, Tel. 51067, Telex 35102). Just up the beach at Legian is the **Legian Beach Hotel** ($38-$40, Tel. 51711, Telex 35104). All three of these hotels are popular with budget travellers, young people and families.

Ubud

About one hour's drive from the beach resorts, up in the mountains is the village of Ubud (pronounced 'Oo-bood'). There are no luxury-class hotels, but the attraction of staying here is the feeling that you are part of Balinese life. The natural beauty (perfect for walks) and the active artists' community make it a unique place to visit.

To get to Ubud it is easiest to hire your own taxi, *bemo* or mini-bus at the beach or at the airport. Once in Ubud you can walk around, take a *bemo* or arrange for a car and driver through your guest house. In Ubud accommodation is usually in a small guest house with several rooms and verandas in Balinese style. There are also homestays, where you have a room within a family's walled-in compound.

Because there are no phones in Ubud, write ahead for reservations and, if you've received no reply, just go there and visit a few places until you find one that suits your fancy.

Ananda Cottages (P.O. Box 205, Denpasar, $15 per person) is owned by Pak Pageh, a former secretary to the king of Ubud. He is a gentle person who speaks good English and is very interested in your enjoying your stay in Bali.

If you like he'll share his knowledge of Balinese culture with you and send you in the direction of colourful local ceremonies such as cremations and tooth-filings. He has a very small garden restaurant and Balinese-style rooms overlooking the rice fields. In the back there is a large, individual house set in the rice fields. The house can be rented whole or by the room. Ananda Cottages is a few minutes out of central Ubud in the village of Campuan, across from the worthwhile Nekka Museum.

In the centre of Ubud is **Han Snell's.** This is a little (tiny) hotel with a very good restaurant. All rooms are Balinese style with a garden setting. The $25 per double includes breakfast and tax.

The **Hotel Campuan** has the only hotel pool in Ubud. While the hotel has a dramatic setting on the side of a ravine, and was once the home of the revered painter Walter Spies, the food (included in room price) and cleanliness could be improved upon.

There are numerous homestays which are inexpensive and especially inviting to the young-at-heart traveller who enjoys closer contact with the Balinese people.

Try **Puri Saren,** the king's palace in the middle of Ubud. There's no sign, just ask. Also try **Mumbul Inn, Jati Homestay** or **Munut's Homestay,** which is up on the hill to the left just after the Campuan bridge. Price is $7 per person. It has a restaurant pavilion in the rice fields. Just down the road in Peliaten is the **Puri Mandala.** Ask to stay in their nicest room—$15 a night with loads of charm.

There are some attractive **private homes** for rent in Ubud. One, which is located above the main road in a garden overlooking more rice fields, has a living room, dining room, veranda and two cheerfully decorated bedrooms, one with a large red Balinese umbrella over the bed. The bathrooms are Western style and new, with individual gardens in them. Rent, including breakfast, is $50-$60 per night. They can sleep six. For reservations write to Ni Wayan Murni, Murni's Warung, Ubud, Bali. You can also enquire about reservations when you get there. Ask at Murni's Restaurant.

The private cottages at **Rumah Ganesha** are also delightful, with beautiful garden and swimming pool. The homes are for rent when the owners are away (most of the time). Reservations can be haphazard. Try writing ahead to Pak Ambara, c/o Segara Village Hotel, P.O. Box 91, Denpasar, Tel. 8407. If this doesn't work, go to the Rumah Ganesha (ask for directions at Murni's Restaurant) and make arrangements with the caretaker. About $50 per night.

Restaurants

Eating in Bali is a pleasure, partly because the waiters and waitresses are so gracious and partly because the garden setting and Balinese style of most restaurants is so charming. There are usually frangipani or hibiscus

blooms on the tables, and the menus list a mix of Chinese, Indonesian and Western dishes. Cooking is usually tasty but rarely gourmet.

In Sanur there are many restaurants and you can walk up and down the beach to a different one every lunch and dinner. The Kul-Kul has a light menu at lunch and especially good seafood at dinner. The Kuri Putih is known for its low prices ($2 for barbecued shrimp!), anxious-to-please staff and folk singers. Also good are the Telaga Naga (across from the Hyatt) and the Swastika II. Pizza and sate are good at the La Taverna Hotel's restaurant. There is a quiet, lovely setting at the restaurant of the Tanjung Sari Hotel. Be careful not to get too full on the warm roasted cocktail peanuts.

If you are in the mood for the big time and high prices, visit the elegant restaurants at the Hyatt Hotel and the Bali Beach Hotel. Their cultural shows and dinners run about $20 per person. If you stay up all night discoing or watching the moonbeams over the beach, there are 24-hour coffee shops at the Hyatt and the Bali Beach.

In Kuta probably the most popular restaurant is Poppie's. Open for lunch, dinner and in between, Poppie's serves freshly blended mango and papaya drinks, fish chowder and a terrific fresh fruit and yoghurt bowl. A Kuta classic!

Also try Lenny's, which is known for its excellent seafood. Other possibilities are Kuta Kayu and Made's Warung, where the local 'in crowd' hangs out. Pertamina Cottages has an expensive Western-style indoor dining room and the Oberoi Hotel has a romantic outdoor dining pavilion.

In Ubud a must is Murni's. This favourite sits at the side of the road just before the bridge to Campuan. It's a tiny place with bamboo furniture, and you overlook a small gorge while you eat. Fresh fruit drinks, nasi campus (mixed rice) and, for breakfast, scrambled eggs with bacon, onion and cheese. Murni is a kind woman with a reputation for a contributing community spirit and good healthy home-style cooking. Closed on Wednesdays.

The Cafe Lotus is also casual and overlooks a large blooming lotus garden. The owner cooked her way through art school in Europe and the resulting menu is special — European chocolate cake, home-made fettucine, garlic prawns and orange cake.

Han Snell's garden restaurant is nice. Griya has delicious chicken. All these places make a nice stop during a day trip to Ubud or for a meal while you are staying there.

Restaurants along the wayside when you are spending a day sightseeing are well known to the tour guides and drivers who take you to them. The food is good and the views are usually memorable. They are Puri Suling at Goa Gajah Elephant Cave, Kintamani and Puri Selera at Kintamani, Tampaksiring Restaurant on the road to Tampaksiring, Bukit Jambul on the way to Besakih, **Ramayana Palace** at Klungkung and **Taman Ayun** at Mengwi. If you will be going way off the regular tourist track you can take along a box lunch from your hotel.

Balinese specialties: Delicious local fruits (banana, papaya, mango, *nangka, salak* and *jeruk Bali*) are served as fruit salad or blended into fruit drinks. There is an excellent mild local fish known as *tengiri*, and lobster, prawns and turtle are often on the menu. Turtle makes a delicious *sate*. Because Bali is Hindu, without Muslim cooking restrictions, pork *sate* is also usually served.

Other Balinese dishes include Bali pancakes (warm with bananas and syrup), a porridge made of black rice, coconut milk and brown sugar, and *bebek tutu* (smoked duck). *Brem Bali* is the sweet local rice wine.

Nightlife

In the Kuta area just cruise the area until you find a lively bar that suits your fancy. On Sanur there are discos: the Matahari at the Hyatt and the Number 1 Disco. Tucked away in a little bungalow at the Tanjung Sari Hotel is Rumours, a quiet little place where you can read, play backgammon and talk in a living-room atmosphere where music is played. Fifty cents entrance fee for non-guests.

All the big hotels (Hyatt, Bali Beach, Sanur Beach, Pertamina Cottages and Oberoi) have regular dinner shows including Balinese dance and music. Prices are $10-$20, and you can telephone ahead to make reservations.

The Abian Restaurant in Sanur has a buffet dinner and *legong* dance for $10, popular with tourists.

The other cultural shows in the villages begin at 6pm so that you are home by 9pm. (See section on *Dances*, page 104.)

People who really know and love Bali get on to the local timetable: up with the roosters at 6am. Since it gets dark at about 6pm they have a shower, change into a colourful caftan, relax over dinner and go to bed early.

Sightseeing

Bali's sights are colourful and easy to explore. Make sure that you take *at least* one day of your holiday to travel in the countryside. The best bet is to arrange through your hotel or one of the travel agencies listed below for a car and driver to take you on various sightseeing trips. The advantage is that you can stop and get out when you see a pretty view, interesting shop or colourful religious ceremony along the way.

Alternatively, sign up for a **bus tour**. The guides will shepherd you around in a large bus or mini-bus. Tour agencies include **Pacto** (Jl. Tanjung Sari, Sanur, Tel. 8247-9) and Bali Lestari Indah (130 Jl. Raya Sanur, Denpasar, Tel. 24000,

26099). Two big tour agencies are **Pacto** (Bali Hyatt, Tel. 8271; Sanur Beach, Tel. 8011; Bali Beach, Tel. 8511; Bali Oberoi, Tel. 5581) and **Bali Travel**(Bali Beach, Tel. 8511; Nusa Dua Beach Hotel; Hyatt, Tel. 8510).

You can rent **motorbikes** at Bakor Motor in Kuta, Ubud and Sanur. You must have an international driver's licence valid for a motorcycle, or a temporary motorcycle driving licence from the Police Department in Denpasar, which can be time-consuming. Motorbikes can be very dangerous on mountain roads. There are always some casualties sitting glumly in the doctors' offices of Bali.

Self-drive cars are also available from Pacto or Bali Wisata Rent-a-Car on the road to Kuta. You must have an international driving licence. Driving is on the left.

Bemos, also called 'colts', are a pleasant way to travel shoulder to shoulder with the Balinese. They are open-backed little mini-buses seating up to eight people. On the main Sanur Beach road you can flag one down (they pass every minute or so), then buzz the buzzer when you reach your destination. Get out and pay the driver Rps 100. Very handy for going up and down the beach.

Bemos also run the route from Sanur into the town of Denpasar. Before leaving your hotel ask for the Indonesian name of the place in Denpasar you want to go to as the *bemo* drivers don't speak English. *Bemos* also travel in the Kuta area, always along set routes. It is possible to travel around the island by *bemo,* but routes are hard to figure out and trips to some areas are infrequent. You can also charter *bemos* for yourself by bargaining with a driver.

If you are in the Denpasar area you can take a short ride around town in an old-fashioned horse and buggy known as a *delman.* Prices must be agreed upon before the trip.

The sights: Every tour agent and private driver will have a standard tour list to show you with prices. The following are the classic tours, listed with average times and prices. They are *all* worth taking.

Kintamani Tour

If you only have one day to tour, this is *the* tour to take. It begins with the Barong dance in a temple at Batubulan. Stop at the craft villages along the way: Celuk (gold and silver), Batuan (weaving), Mas (woodcarving) and Ubud (painting). See the craftsmen at work and have an opportunity to shop. See Tampaksiring's holy spring temple and the president's summer residence. Lunch at Kintamani, 5,000 feet above sea level. Marvellous view of active volcano, Mt Batur, and its crater lake. Return home along the coast, stopping at the 13th century temple of Bangli.

(Tour: 150 kilometres, 7 hours)

Bali trance dance with magical knives (kris)

Besakih Tour
Drive to Besakih, called the 'Mother Temple' of Bali, the biggest and
most sacred temple of all, situated on the slopes of Mount Agung, 3,142
metres above sea level. Return via Klungkung; the ancient capital of
Bali, where you can see the painted ceilings showing heaven and hell at
the Kerta Gosa Palace of Justice, and shop for antiques.
(Tour: 140 kilometres, 6 hours)

Mengwi-Sangeh Tour
Visit the Taman Ayun or Royal Temple of Bali at Mengwi and Sangeh,
with its green moss-covered temple courtyards filled with monkey
families. Beware of monkeys who snatch your glasses and earrings.
(Tour: 70 kilometres, 5 hours)

Tanah Lot Tour
Take a private car to this cliffside temple where enormous waves crash
hundreds of feet below you. Especially impressive at sunset. This can be
tied in with a visit to Kuta Beach.
(Tour: 75 kilometres, 4 hours)

Tenganan Tour
Tenganan is an old walled village where the Bali Age, the original pre-
Hindu Balinese race, live in isolation. They are famous for their double-

Balinese style guest cottage, Ubud

ikat cloth and adhere to their old customs. On the way, stop at Klungkung and pass through barren land devastated by a volcanic eruption in 1963. Stop at the Bat Cave Temple, the Kusamba fishing harbour and the primitive salt-making huts.
(Tour: 8 hours, 130 kilometres)

Other Interesting Sights

If you have a private car and driver ask to see some of the following, which can sometimes be added into your standard tours. One interesting sight is a **Balinese home,** not a single structure but a series of pavilions set in a walled courtyard. The parents live in one pavilion and there are other pavilions for grandparents and children. Elsewhere in the compound are the rice barn, pigpen, kitchen and family temples.

Your hotel information desk can tell you when a major **cremation** is taking place. These are very elaborate affairs which are held well after the death of the individual. Observe the preparation of offerings, of foods for guests (roasted pig), and see the enormous cremation towers burned with the body inside, freeing the spirit for union with the cosmos, a cause for joyous celebration.

Balinese temples are always beautiful to visit during the day of the **temple odalan.** Throughout the year they are tranquil havens, a series of brick courtyards decorated with stone carvings. Every year (210 days on the

Balinese calendar) every temple celebrates its *odalan*, or temple holiday. People from the area stream to the sanctuary, wearing their brightest finery and parading along the roads to the temple with metre-high offerings of fruits and flowers. Music and prayers fill the temple. Every hotel and guest house in Bali has a black-and-white calendar showing which temples are celebrating their *odalan* on a given day, so you should be able to plan a trip to one of these interesting ceremonies during your visit. Make sure that you wear a sash (important temple dress), and never stand on the pavilions in the temples.

Galungan and Kuningan are the best time to visit Bali. During this 'holy week', which takes place every 210 days, Bali's villages and temples are alive with music, dance and decoration to honour the gods during their stay on earth.

Details on other festivals, holidays and travel tips are crammed into the informative *ABC of Bali*, a free handbook available at the tourist information offices at the airport or at the Kanwil Pariwisata Bali on Jalan Raya Puputan, Kompleks Niti Mandala, Denpasar (the main tourist office). This excellent publication was written by John Darling, an anthropologist and filmmaker who lives in Bali.

Museums

The **Museum of Bali** on Jalan Mayor Wisnu on the eastern side of Puputan Square in Denpasar houses an excellent collection of Balinese art and artefacts from prehistoric to modern times. Open daily 8am-2pm except Fridays, 8am-11am, and Mondays when it is closed all day.

The **Museum Puri Lukisan** in Ubud is an excellent collection of modern Balinese paintings and carvings in a lovely hillside garden setting. Open daily. Also see **Lempad's House** in Ubud.

The **Museum Le Mayeur** is the former house of the late Belgian painter Le Mayeur, who moved to Bali in 1932 and married the beautiful *legong* dancer Ni Polok. Her daughter will show you around their house, which is filled with his paintings.

The **Nekka Museum** in Campuan, near Ubud, is a fine collection of modern Balinese paintings, some for sale. The best works are in the permanent collection.

Dances

Another absolute must during a stay in Bali is to see the typical Balinese dances. Some of the dances were originally choreographed by village people to please the gods during temple festivals, to aid in the ritual cleansing of the island or simply to amuse. They are almost all accompanied by the gong and metallaphone *gamelan* orchestra to a lively beat which is far brighter than the Javanese *gamelan*.

Today these dances continue to be performed in the villages and are important parts of village ceremonial life. However, some of the best troupes perform at regularly scheduled tourist dances. Among the best are the following: The **Barong Dance** is performed at Batubulan every day from 9 to 10am. This is a hit with all ages. Portions of the *Ramayana* story come alive with dreadful demons, mournful princes, playful monkeys and pompous prime ministers. Good (the enormous shaggy mythical lion named Barong) and evil (the long-nailed witch Rangda) struggle. Also part of this always popular show is the *legong* dance, where two beautiful maidens decked out in flower headpieces and golden adornments sway, their fingers fluttering and their eyes flashing to the beat of the music. The performance ends with a trance dance, where dancers flail *kris* daggers. The trance is only simulated, but in the real village dances trances are actually induced.

The **Fire Dance** is performed every Monday, Tuesday and Friday night from 6 to 7pm in the town of Bona. Here the illusion is not faked—it's real. A bonfire is built out of coconut husks and the coals are scattered across the courtyard. Suddenly a dancer on a hobby horse bursts through the coals, dancing on the hot embers. Amazing! Also part of the evening's show are a *kecak* dance and a dance of two young, supposedly entranced, girls.

The **Kecak Dance** is another Balinese specialty. Held every evening from 6 to 7pm at the Ayodya Pura on the road between Denpasar and Sanur, this dance includes a cast of 100 men in a monkey chorus. They click and shout, imitating the forest sounds of monkeys as a choral background for the dancers who portray the drama of Rama, his love Sinta and the evil Rahwana.

Kecak dances are also held at the Art Centre on Jalan Nusa Indah in Denpasar every day from 6 to 7pm, in Ubud at the Banjar Padang Tegal on Sundays at 6pm, and in Kuta and Legian.

A *Wayang Kulit* puppet performance in English is given at the Mars Hotel in Sanur every Sunday, Tuesday and Thursday from 6 to 7pm. The puppeteer holds his puppets up to the screen, creating a lifelike shadow. You are free to sit in the audience section facing the screen or to wander backstage to see the puppeteer at work.

All the above-mentioned dances are well done and quite authentic. But the most exciting way to see a performance is in the villages, where the performers are performing only for their village's satisfaction and ceremonial life. To find out about these performances, ask your hotel for information or check with your tour guide. You must show real interest, otherwise they'll send you in the direction of the usual tourist dances.

Shopping

Bali is a wonderful place to shop. There's a wealth of handicrafts that range from cheap to expensive but are always reasonably priced compared

with prices for handcrafted work back home. There are shops everywhere. The main tourist shops are found on the road between the beach areas (Sanur and Kuta) and Ubud. Always bargain. Each village along this road has a specialty, as you'll read below.

Kuta is bulging with shops selling bamboo wind chimes, baskets, paintings, sculpture and colourful clothing. Sanur also has shops of clothes and handicrafts along the beach and roadside. The Hyatt Hotel has the highest quality shops, with a full selection of things from all over Bali. And now, for the things that will tempt you—

Bali Clothes: Everyone buys something new to wear. These clothes are calculated to make you feel ten years younger and 20 percent more cheerful than you already are. Prices will also keep a smile on your face. Batik shirts (the shop-owner can make them in your size overnight) are $5-$10. Bright caftans $5-$15. Dresses with lacy designs at the neck $8-$40. Brightly coloured patched jackets $10 here, $60 in New York. Teeny-weeny bikinis $2-$10.

Woodcarvings: Painted wooden knick-knacks are always fanciful and fun. Fish napkin rings frogs playing musical instruments ($5) and carved ducks. In the villages of Mas, Jati and Nyuhkuning you can stop to see workshops where fine woodcarvers create sculpture, mobiles and doors. Two of the best carvers are Ida Bagus Nyana and his son Ida

Besakih Temple on Mount Agung

Bagus Tilem. The village of Pengosekan turns out roughly crafted polychrome mirror frames covered with birds and flowers that are just about irresistible.

Stone Sculpture: You will soon realise that the Balinese are keen stone carvers. Every temple is richly carved. Every single bridge in Bali has four protective *raksasas* (demons) guarding it. The stone carving village is Batubulan. It is the same town where the famous Barong dance intrigues tourists every morning. Prices for a *raksasa* two metres tall are about $35-$50. The shop-owner can arrange for shipping to your home.

The stonecarver Cemul works in Ubud on the same street as Han Snell's Restaurant. His fanciful animal sculptures have been shown internationally, though he remains a modest man.

Gold and Silver: Once specialising in gold *kris* handles and hair ornaments for royal dancers, today the craftsmen make jewellery for sale to tourists in the shops in the village of Celuk. Two of the biggest shops are Dewi Karnia and Sura. Bargain.

Masks: Masks of frogs, prime ministers, fat-lipped coarse characters, sweet young damsels and white-haired old men are all used in the Balinese dances known as *topeng*. You can buy these masks for as little as $5 in the curio shops in Kuta, Sanur and Ubud. Really fine masks are carved in the village of Mas by such masters as Ida Bagus Glodok, Ambara and Ida Bagus Sutarja.

Paintings: The Ubud area is the place to buy Bali's paintings. The inexpensive 'primitives' of rice fields in blue and green are painted by children in Campuan and Penestenan. Works of Bali's finer painters can be seen in the Nekka Gallery in Ubud and Campuan, and in the workshops of I. Bagus Made behind the Oka Kartini Inn, Sobrat and Ida Bagus Nadera in Padangtegal and I. Gusti Ketut Kobot in Pengosekan.

When you visit the Palace of Justice in Klungkung you'll see fine examples of ochre-coloured *wayang* style paintings on the roof of the palace. Hawkers at the gate sell new *wayang* paintings. Finer examples by old masters are available in the village of Kamasan. The hawkers also sell *lontar* palm manuscripts, little 'books' fashioned from palm leaves and etched with pictures of traditional legends.

Temple Decorations: In the Kumbasari art market in Denpasar or along the roadside in the town of Sukawati you can find a plentiful supply of temple decorations. These include the gold and brightly coloured umbrellas, hanging decorations of Chinese coins, mirrors and hot pink yarn and *kain prada* material, brightly coloured and painted with gold.

Baskets: In the markets along the roadside as you make your tours into the countryside you will see baskets large and small at reasonable prices ($1-$25). There's a good selection in Kuta and in the village of Bona.

Terracotta and Ceramics: Very cheap and cute are the fanciful terracotta ashtrays and stylised human figures which you can find in the Kumbasari Art Market in Denpasar, where you poke around among the piles in the darkly-lit bazaar. Or buy them at the fancy Earth and Fire (Sari Bumi) ceramics store in the Hyatt shopping arcade. Also see their charming ceramic plates, ashtrays and casserole dishes in whimsical designs. They are made at the Jangala kiln down the beach from the Hyatt. Just about every nice hotel and restaurant seems to be using their distinctive blue wares.

Bamboo Furniture: High-style, huge furniture created of cushions and wide bamboo is designed by Linda Garland, one of the island's excellent artists. She also designs umbrellas painted with soft botanical designs and exotic glass coffee tables. To find her, ask at the Cafe Lotus in Ubud.

Shipping Home: It's best to take your things home in your luggage. Large pieces can be shipped home, though. Ask your hotel for the name of a reliable agent or try Elteha. The shop-owner may be able to handle the shipping for you, if you pay him in advance. As with shipping anywhere, be careful. Snafus can occur.

Sports

Swimming is, of course, very popular at the many hotel pools of Kuta, Sanur and Nusa Dua. For a small charge non-hotel guests may use the facilities. Swimming can be rough at Kuta Beach, so observe the warning signs. Swimming at Sanur Beach is only good for half the day when the tide is in. This is not a reason to avoid Sanur, however, as you can stay quite happy with part-time beaching and part-time sightseeing and pool swimming.

Sanur Beach has colourful **outrigger boats** with upside-down triangular sails which take you out for trips along the shore for about one hour. The price is fixed by the co-operative of sailors. These well-tanned men will sail you out to the reef where you can **snorkel** over the side and children can bob around the boat, hanging on to the outriggers for safety.

If you want to sail to Turtle Island (Pulau Serangan), go down to the Sanur Beach Hotel and hire a boat at the beach there, cutting sailing time down to about one hour. At the island there is a temple and you can have a Coke at the snack stand.

Boating at the Hyatt Hotel beach. Waterskiing, windsurfing and topper sailing. The Tanjung Sari Hotel has windsurfers and the Nusa Dua Beach Hotel has windsurfing, sailing and snorkelling.

Surfing at Kuta and Legian beaches. Though **diving** is wonderful in other parts of Indonesia, such as in the Thousand Islands off Jakarta, it's not really available in Bali. For those with the time and money, you can rent a 58-foot **sailing** ketch for the day or for extended five-day

Sending the ashes to sea at a Balinese cremation

diving trips.

One of Indonesia's most beautiful **golf** courses is the Bali Handara Golf Club at Bedugul, about one hour from the beach areas. You can arrange for transportation there through the hotel travel agents. Prices include taxi, green fees, caddy and rental of clubs. Golf carts available. For those who want to do nothing but golf in Bali, stay at the club by making reservations ahead (Bali Handara Country Club, P.O. Box 324, Denpasar, Tel. 3046, 6419).

There is a nine-hole public golf course and a mini-golf course at the Bali Beach Hotel.

Horseback riding on the beach can be arranged through the La Taverna Hotel on Sanur Beach. **Bowling** at the Bali Beach Hotel. **Tennis** and **squash** fans will enjoy the new facilities at the Nusa Dua Beach Hotel, which also has a jogging track, health club and gymnasium. Tennis also at the Bali Hyatt, Pertamina Cottages and Bali Beach Hotel.

Final Tips

Books and some medicines are available in the drugstores of the big hotels. **Drugstores** (called *apotik*) are on the airport road to Kuta and at Farmisari in Sanur. A large, modern **grocery store** called Galael's is on Jalan Imam Bonjol, the main road out of Kuta towards Denpasar. There's a

Entrance to a Balinese temple

doctor in the Bali Beach Hotel. **Film** is widely available. **Massage** is an Indonesian skill. Arrange through hotel desk. Very, very relaxing.

Sumatra

Indonesia's second largest island, Sumatra, is a treasure-house of natural resources and diverse cultural influences. The landscape of the island is varied and often spectacularly beautiful. There is a north-south volcanic range known as the Bukit Barisan. Sumatra is peppered with 300 volcanoes, nine of which are active. There are many rivers and lakes. With annual rainfall of 77-100 inches, the land has lush vegetation and jungle, though roads are often flooded.

Indonesia is well aware of the vast natural resources of the island. Private and government-owned estates are increasing production of rubber, palm oil, cacao and sugar.

Despite this natural wealth, the population of Sumatra remains small by comparison with neighbouring Java. Twenty-eight million people are spread out over an island 1,800 kilometres long and 400 kilometres wide.

There is great cultural diversity in Sumatra, a rich source of interest for the tourist and armchair traveller. At the northern tip of Sumatra is the strongly-Muslim province of **Aceh.** Women who travel in this region find it is best not to be forward with the somewhat aggressive men, and are careful to appear conservative.

The **Batak** people live around the Lake Toba area of North Sumatra. For centuries they were isolated in the highlands, holding on to their animistic beliefs and practising cannibalism as recently as the last century. Although Christian missionaries had little success in the north, they were successful in the Batak region. Today most Bataks are Christian, although some still maintain some of their animistic beliefs.

The Bataks live in distinctive houses built on stilts with high, saddle-shaped roofs. The main posts, walls and gable ends carry carved decorations. Their life is mainly agricultural and their traditional textiles are sombre in colour and relatively simple, an example of their relative isolation from outside artistic and cultural influences. The Bataks can be divided into several subgroups: Toba, Karo, Pakpak, Simalungun, Angkola and Mandailing. While each group speaks a different dialect, they can understand one another.

Further to the south, in western Sumatra about midway down the island live the **Minangkabau** people, who gather in the cities of Padang and Bukittinggi. They too live in distinctive homes with horn-shaped roofs and are known for their matrilineal kinship system.

More isolated people live on the island of **Nias** off the western coast of Sumatra. Nias is a popular stop for cruise ships. Shiploads of camera-toting tourists disembark to see traditional houses built on stilts surrounding the village square and to attend performances of traditional war dances complete with armour and shields and the impressive stone-jumping ritual. Aside from visiting by cruise ship, travel in Nias is difficult.

History

As early as the 7th century there was mention of the powerful Hindu kingdom of Srivijaya, which was established near the modern-day city of Palembang in South Sumatra. Palembang was the heart of the empire, which had a powerful navy that controlled the Straits of Malacca and the Sunda Straits between Sumatra and Java.

Muslim kingdoms began to be established along Sumatra's coast in the 13th century, and Islam spread throughout the island, except for some of the isolated areas where people still remain essentially animists or have become Christians, as among the Batak.

In 1292 Marco Polo was the first European to visit Sumatra. The Portuguese came to Sumatra in 1509 and gained control of the port of Malacca, on the Malay Peninsula across the straits from Sumatra. In 1569 the Dutch came, setting up commercial establishments in Sumatra, and in

1685 the British established trading posts in Bengkulu, Padang and North Sumatra.

Despite these foreign influences, the indigenous rulers continued to be powerful and to wage war with the foreign intruders. In the highlands of West Sumatra the Dutch fought against the Padris, or orthodox Muslims, who were engaged in civil war against the less orthodox Muslims. When the Padris were defeated, the Dutch held on to territory belonging to the southern Batak tribes as part of their spoils.

Travel in Sumatra

The city of Medan in northeastern Sumatra is an international port of entry into Indonesia. Medan is linked by air with Jakarta, Singapore and Penang by regularly scheduled flights and a continuous ferry service. The flying time to Jakarta from Medan is two hours; from Singapore to Medan, one hour; from Penang to Medan, 20 minutes.

Bus travel is possible, but remember that distances in Sumatra are long. Some roads tend to be flooded, and buses are packed with people and loud music. The trans-Sumatra highway, which goes from north to south, is nearing completion. For the very adventurous traveller there is a weekly sea voyage from Jakarta to Medan on Pelni Lines that takes about 36 hours.

The *Princess Mahsuri* is the luxurious way to visit Nias and Padang, while the SS *Kerinci* does the Jakarta–Padang run. See details in *Tours and Cruises*, page 20.

The most **popular tourist destinations** in Sumatra are Lake Toba and Bukittinggi, both of which you can visit on your own or through one of the many tours offered by foreign travel agents in Singapore, or by Pacto Ltd and Garuda Airlines. In Medan the Pacto office is at Jl. Palang Merah 28/1, Tel. 28828. In Padang (near Bukittinggi) Pacto is at 142 Jl. Yamin, Tel. 23780.

To go to **Lake Toba,** fly to Medan and hire a car and driver for the three-hour trip to Prapat, a city on the lake shore. You can stay in Prapat or, better still, take a public ferry or private launch across the lake to the enormous Samosir island. Spend from two to four days there swimming, hiking, touring the traditional houses and villages, shopping for textiles and crafts and listening to the vibrant Batak music of this beautiful, peaceful area. Return via the same route or stop overnight in the mountain resort of Brastagi. Head back to Medan the next day for some sightseeing and an optional trip to the Orang-utan Rehabilitation Centre in Bukit Lawang.

To make the **Bukittinggi** trip, fly to Padang and hire a car and driver for the two-hour trip to Bukittinggi, spending several days there exploring this beautiful and culturally rich area before flying home.

Anyone planning to live in Sumatra or wishing to travel extensively

Gang Bengkok Mosque in Medan, Sumatra

there should order a copy of *Living in Sumatra* published by the Parents' Association of the Medan International School, Brastagi Road at Jl. Tali Air, Medan, North Sumatra (Tel. 20398). It gives useful information for residents and tips on hotels, guest houses and sights all over Sumatra.

Medan

Medan is the capital city and trading centre of North Sumatra. With a population of more than one million, it is Indonesia's fourth largest city. The port of Medan is at Belawan, 26 kilometres north, where there is a ferry link with Penang. Most international tourists arrive in Medan at Polonia Airport and, after a brief look at the sights, continue on their journey to Lake Toba. Although they are open to the noise and dust, the easiest and most colourful way to get around Medan is by *becak* pedicab. Most things in Medan are close to one another. There are taxi stands at the airport, the Tiara, Danau Toba, Polonia and Garuda Plaza hotels and at the railway station. Settle on the price before you enter. The driver can take you to Lake Toba or on a city tour.

Sightseeing in Medan should certainly include the **Mesjid Raya** (Great Mosque) on Jalan Sisingamangaraja, built at the beginning of the 20th century and one of Indonesia's most beautiful structures. Another important stop is the **Istana Sultan Deli** (the palace of the sultan of Deli) on Jalan Katamso, built in 1888. Medan was formerly part of the sultanate of Deli. Read about the Chinese-Indonesian lifestyle in Medan and visits to the sultan's home in the early part of the 20th century in *Memories of a Nonya* by Queeny Chang.

A tour around the **Lapangan Merdeka,** or Freedom Square, will show many lovely old colonial buildings. Visit the mansion of the late Chinese millionaire Chong A. Fie on Jalan Yani. The oldest mosque in Medan, built in the 17th century, is the **Gang Bengkok Mosque.** History buffs may wish to visit the **Medan Garnizoen,** Jl. Kapt. Maulana Lubis, which was a Dutch colonial army fort built in 1873. The **Taman Margasatwa Zoo,** four kilometres out of the city centre, should be visited during the week, when it is less crowded than on weekends. Of some interest may be the **Cultural Centre** Tapian Daya, Jl. Binjei Km. 6, which has some traditional performances.

If you would rather be playing **golf** than sightseeing, try the Nicotiana and Padang courses, both good nine-hole courses hacked out of the jungle outside town.

The **Bahorok Orang-utan Rehabilitation Centre** is a two-hour drive from Medan in Bukit Lawang, about 80 kilometres away. It is situated in the Langkat reserve, and was opened in 1973 with the aim of returning the protected orang-utans to their natural habitat. To visit the reserve each

Karo Batak house in Brastagi, Sumatra

person entering must obtain a pass (a simple process) by presenting his or
her passport at the PPA (Indonesian Nature Conservation Office) at Jl.
Sungei Galang 26, Medan. The drive to the reserve takes about two hours,
passing through forests and rubber plantations. You may enter the reserve
only in a group at 8am and 3.30pm every day. Once you arrive you will
walk about 20 minutes to the boat crossing and the entrance to the reserve.
The river is clear and good for wading or swimming while you have a
picnic nearby. Register at the park ranger's hut. He will help you across the
river on a hollowed-out log canoe and lead the group of visitors along a
clear-cut path up the mountain to see the feeding of the semi-wild orang-
utans. This is a nice day trip by hire car from Medan.

Shopping

Visit Medan's **antique and curio** shops along Jalan Yani, such as Toko
Bali at No.68 and Rufino at No.64. They sell new 'Ming' porcelain, woven
rattan bracelets, Palembang red lacquer boxes, Dutch-style hanging lamps
and pounded brass mirrors. See the **gold** jewellery at Toko Mas Makmur
on Jl. Yani V, Tel. 25734. At Pasar Ikan Lama (old fish market) you'll find
textiles galore. There's ready-made batik at Danar Hadi (Jl. Arifin 131, Tel.
323773) and Batik Semar, Jl. Jend. Yani 128, and road **maps** at Toko Buku
Deli on Jalan Yani. A first-class artist who specialises in high-quality **batik
pictures** is Azis, Jl. Sutrisno, Berlian 494T. This is art, not junk.

Hotels in Medan

The newest hotel, opened in 1982, is the Hotel Tiara Medan (★★★★ Jl.
Cut Mutiah, Tel. 516000, Telex 5172). It has 800 rooms, swimming pool,
shopping arcade, function rooms, tennis and squash and a Clark Hatch
physical fitness centre. The Danau Toba International (★★★★ Jl. Imam
Bonjol 17, Tel. 327000, Telex 51167) has a pool, bowling and gardens. The
Polonia (★★★ Jl. Jend Sudirman, Tel. 325300, Telex 51376) has 200 rooms
and a pool.

Restaurants in Medan

The Tiara Hotel has a nice coffee shop and grillroom. The Bali Plaza
Restaurant (Jl. Kumango 1A) serves Chinese food and has good corn and
crab soup. For informal atmosphere with a local flavour try Lynn's Bar on
Jalan Jend. Yani, where steaks are reasonably priced, or the Batik Cafe on
Jalan Pemuda, which specialises in lobster but is not fancy. Try Chinese
food at the Tip Top Restaurant on Jalan Jend. Yani 92A. The best Padang
(spicy) food in Medan is at Rumah Makan Garuda on Jalan Pemuda. Go
early at lunchtime when the food is fresh.

Lake Toba

The main reason most tourists visit North Sumatra is to make the trip to
Lake Toba. Nine hundred metres above sea level, the lake is the largest lake

in Southeast Asia, some 80 kilometres long and formed by volcanic eruptions. It is beautiful and clear, with good coves for swimming and a shoreline banked with pine trees, beaches, slopes and cliffs. At the centre of the lake is the island of Samosir, which covers 392 square miles, about the same size as Singapore. Samosir is known as the original home of the tribe of Toba Bataks, and the island offers royal tombs, Batak houses, stone carvings, walks, hikes and swimming. Churches dot the landscape, as 80 percent of the people are Christian mixed with much older animistic beliefs.

Tour agents in Medan hotels can arrange one, two and three-day tours to Lake Toba for you, or you can hire a car and driver at your hotel to drive you to Prapat, the main town on the shores of the lake. (See Sumatra introduction, page 113.) There are two routes to Lake Toba. The first route takes about three hours and goes through Tebbing Tinggi and Pemantang Siantar. This route is a new two-lane road which goes through beautiful rubber and palm oil plantations, perfect for a picnic along the way. The tour agent can arrange for you to have lunch at Pabatu, a state-owned palm oil plantation.

The alternate route to Lake Toba, which you might try on the way back, takes about six hours and goes through Brastagi (where you can spend the night) and Kabanjahe to Prapat. This road is very scenic though the mountain driving, with hairpin turns, is more nerve-racking than the shorter route. There are, however, several interesting sights along the way. About 40 kilometres from Medan on the way to Brastagi is **Sibolangit**, a botanical reserve with many species of tropical plants and a nice place for a picnic. Twelve kilometres before you reach Brastagi is **Sikulikap Waterfall.** It is 300 metres from the main road along a steep path but is worth the walk to see the 120-foot waterfall.

Brastagi is a mountain resort 1½ hours from Medan. It has an abundance of flowers, vegetables and fruits, the most famous of which is the marquisa passion fruit. There are also persimmons, pomegranates and strawberries. In former times Brastagi was the weekend resort of European planters. Today you can play golf and ride small ponies. Stay overnight at a delightful old colonial-style hotel, the **Bukit Kubu** (★ Jl. Sempurna 2, Tel. 2 Brastagi) which is set in the grounds of the golf course. There is a lovely view from the dining room and good Indonesian food. The **Rudang Hotel** (★★ Jl. Sempurna, Tel. 43 Brastagi) is medium-priced, new and more modern than the Bukit Kubu. The food here is also good and the restaurant clean.

From Brastagi you can see Mount Sibayak, Mount Sinabung and Gundaling Hill, where there are giant totem poles. The adventurous will enjoy a two to three-hour hike up **Mount Sibayak.** You can hire a guide at the base. The path is clear and tennis shoes are adequate.

After leaving Brastagi, five kilometres away on the road to Kabanjahe is

Megalithic stone tables and chairs on Samosir island, Lake Toba

the village of **Raya,** where there is a museum of Karo Batak artefacts,
ceremonial daggers and traditional woven cloth.

Perhaps the best sightseeing is in the village of **Lingga,** five kilometres
north of Kabanjahe. This is a village of large, painted and decorated Batak
houses which are still in active use today. The interior of each house
consists of a cooking area and a long hall partitioned off to accommodate
married couples. You must have a local guide accompany you into the
village, and you should tip him. In the village of **Pematung Purba** you will
see a village used by the Simalungan Bataks where the house of the tribal
chief has been preserved for more than two centuries.

The **Si Piso-Piso Waterfall** is a narrow waterfall in the Karo highlands
that drops into a gorge. It is about an hour's walk off the main road
between Kabanjahe and Pematung Purba at Tongging.

The goal of both these routes described above is **Lake Toba. Prapat,** 176
kilometres from Medan, is the main tourist town on the shores of Lake
Toba. It is a mountain and lake resort with many hotels and facilities for
water sports such as boating, waterskiing and swimming. Traditional dance
and music performances can be organised and horses are available for
riding. Most of the hotels are located on the shore, with one exception.

It is more pleasant, however, to stay on the island itself, as the
atmosphere is more peaceful. From your base on the island take a day tour

by boat to the villages listed below. From Prapat travel to the island of Samosir via hired motorboat (about $40 for half a day), or take a regular public ferry. The Andilo Booking Office at Jalan Balige 37, the main road coming into Prapat, sells ferry tickets. The cost from Prapat to Tomok or Tuk Tuk is about Rps 1,000. There is another ferry point in Prapat at Tiga Raja in the market area at the other side of town.

The trip across the lake takes about half an hour to the village of **Tomok,** the main entry point to Samosir island. The traditional houses in Tomok are beautifully carved and have saddle-shaped roofs. Near the village is the tomb of King Sidabutar, who lived 200 years ago. There are also other megalithic tombs and sarcophagi in the vicinity. After visiting Tomok, go by boat, by *bemo* (little mini-truck) or hike to some of the other villages along the coast of Samosir island.

Down the peninsula from Tomok is the village of **Tuk Tuk,** a quiet, peaceful place to stay where the swimming is excellent. Continuing on around the peninsula you'll come to the village of **Ambarita** (13 kilometres from Prapat) where there is a stone court of kings in front of the traditional houses. Chairs of stone surround the table where the king held court. Further along the shore is **Tao island,** a tiny place off the shore of Samosir that is perfect for relaxation and privacy. There is good swimming here and waterskiing is available. It's an excellent place to have lunch while touring Samosir.

Take the ten-minute boat ride back to Samosir island to the village of **Simanindo.** Here the former king's house is one of the most outstanding Batak houses on the island. There is a pleasant cafe with good food.

Hotels in Lake Toba

In Prapat there are many hotels along the lakeside. The Danau Toba Hotel (★★ Jl. Samosir 17, Tel. 41583, Telex 51167 HDTI MDN) has especially nice rooms on the upper level facing the water. The Hotel Sinar Baru on Jalan Barisan is medium-priced and friendly. Away from the lake on a hill with a magnificent view is the Wisma Pertamina International, which has a pool, tennis and nine-hole golf course, though at times it seems somewhat empty and isolated.

The following hotels are located on Samosir island. In Tomok try the Toba Beach Hotel (Medan Tel. 515562, Telex 51605 SUKMA MDN), which has good Indonesian food and rooms arranged like traditional Batak houses. Top recommendation for your stay in Lake Toba is the Toledo Inn in Tuk Tuk, which has cottages, swimming and paddleboats for rent. The Tuk Tuk Hotel is comfortable, modern and much like a motel. Reservations through the Medan office (Tel. 325773). On some days there is a mini-bus that takes guests to Simanindo, Pangururan, Ambarita and the hot springs on the mainland.

The Carolina Hotel in Tuk Tuk has a beach and Batak-style cottages.

Bathrooms are Indonesian style with cold water, and you will have to bring along your own extra sheets, toilet paper and soap. Pleasant local atmosphere and wholesome food. Reservations through Sukma Wisata in Medan (Tel. 24850).

Shopping in Lake Toba

The best shopping is in Prapat and Tomok, where you will have no trouble finding thick cotton textiles used by the Bataks for sarongs, headdresses or stoles. Prices run $3-$4 for simple ones, $30-$60 for finer examples. Most of these cloths are in sombre blue colours, although some from the Karo highlands are woven with bright reds and pinks on a black background. The textiles are called *ulos*, and they are important Batak gifts at birth and marriage. Some *ulos* have powers to protect their wearers during difficulties in life.

Wood panels are available, carved and painted in the same geometric designs you will recognise on traditional Batak houses. Necklaces, bracelets and belts made from beads, wood and boar tusks are available. Batak calendars carved on pieces of bamboo, and magic wands, are also popular souvenirs.

West Sumatra

The province of West Sumatra is a beautiful area facing the sea, with volcanic mountains, dense jungles and canyons inland. The region is famous as the home of the Minangkabau people, faithful Muslims who are known for their colourful red-and-gold weaving and their distinctive architecture. During your visit you will see traditional *adat* (customary) houses—long rectangular buildings built high on stilts. The interior is sectioned off with a room for each daughter and her husband. The roofs turn upwards at the ends, like sharp, pointed horns. The story goes that long ago the people of West Sumatra were engaged in a battle with the Javanese. It was decided that their differences would be settled by a fight between two buffaloes. The Javanese selected as their representative a huge female buffalo while the Minangkabau chose a tender-looking calf. The outcome was obvious, or so everyone thought. But no. Using their native wit the Minangkabau put poison on the horns of the little calf and, as she went to suckle the much larger animal, her poisoned horns killed it. Hence the name of the people: Minang (victorious) *kabau* (buffalo).

The Minangkabau have a distinctive matrilineal system whereby one's family name and inheritance come through the female line. A man works in his own family's home, only going to spend the night in his wife's family's home. Major family decisions are traditionally made by the wife's brother, although recently more of the family decisions have been transferred to her husband.

Minangkabau men work as farmers, though many have left their

Traditional house of West Sumatra

homeland for the bigger cities and Java in order to seek fame and fortune. They have distinguished themselves in many fields and are responsible for the proliferation of Padang-style restaurants outside their own region. Padang food is noted for its spiciness, and is often served from communal plates piled high in the windows of the restaurants.

The most popular tourist itinerary in West Sumatra is to fly to Padang and do some sightseeing before proceeding onward by car or bus to the beautiful highland city of Bukittinggi, about two hours away. There are many side trips available in the region, all of which can be reached by car rented in Padang or Bukittinggi.

Arrival in West Sumatra

Arrival in West Sumatra is at Tabing Airport, which is 8.5 kilometres from the city of Padang. There are regular flights from Jakarta and Medan. The seaport of Padang is at Teluk Bayur, six kilometres from the centre of town. For information on arrival by ship, see the sections on boats and cruises on page 20.

Padang

Padang is the capital of West Sumatra and the third largest city on the island. It is an attractive town with several interesting sights. The **Padang**

Woodcarver in West Sumatra

Museum is a newly-built museum in traditional Minangkabau style with many objects of cultural and historical interest. Closed Mondays.

Check with your hotel to see if there are any performances of traditional Minang dances being held at the Konservatori Seni Kerawitan (arts centre). You may be able to see performances of *silat*, which combines dance with martial arts.

Visit the government tourist office, BAPPARDA, at Jalan Koto Tinggi 5 for information on the region. Twenty kilometres south of Padang is the beach at the **Bay of Bungus,** which has white sand and is ideal for swimming or watching the fishing boats. You can rent boats to take you to the nearby islands. Take drinks and a picnic along with you.

For shopping in Padang, try Silungkang, Jl. Imam Bonjol 6A for paintings, carvings, textiles and embroideries. Handwoven cloth with gold and silver thread is available at Pasar Raya, the main market.

Hotels in Padang include the Mariani International (★★★ Jl. Bundo Kandung 35, Tel. 22020), which is centrally located and has a swimming pool and veranda. Machudum's (★★ Jl. Hiligoo 43, Tel. 22333), Aldilla (★ Jl. Damar 2, Tel. 23962), which has only fifteen rooms, each with a porch overlooking a garden, and Natour's Hotel Muara (★ Jl. Gereja 3, Tel. 21601).

Bukittinggi

When given a choice of spending time in Padang or in Bukittinggi, most tourists opt for the city of Bukittinggi, a two to two-and-a-half hour ride into the highlands from Padang. You can take an hourly bus or hire a car and driver to take you there. Two helpful travel agencies in Padang are Pacto (Jl. Yamin 142, Tel. 27780) and Nitour (Jl. Hiligoo 41, Tel. 22175). Once you get to Bukittinggi you can arrange local tours at Yani Valley Rama (101 Jl. Yani, Tel. 22740).

On the ride from Padang to Bukittinggi you are surrounded by beautiful scenery as you go up the Anai Valley to the Agam Plateau. On the right side of the highway there is a beautiful lookout area.

Bukittinggi is the cultural and educational centre of the Minangkabau people. It is a beautiful city—sunny, cool and friendly. It is 930 metres above sea level and surrounded by three volcanoes—Sago, Singgalang and Merapi. On the outskirts of town is the beautiful **Ngarai Sianok,** a canyon about 100 metres deep that falls into a green valley with a winding river. Most of the sights of Bukittinggi can be visited on foot or by taking the gaily decorated horse carts that are also popular in Padang.

Sightseeing in Bukittinggi begins at the town's centre of attraction, a clocktower topped with a horn-shaped roof overlooking the market square. Located on the highest hill in town is the **Rumah Adat Baandjuang Museum,** built in traditional Minangkabau style. Behind it is a zoo with a large bird collection and Sumatran wildlife—tigers, orang-utans, bears and miniature buffaloes. **Fort de Kock** was built in 1925 by the Dutch, and from it you can enjoy a view of the town, especially nice in the late afternoons.

Twelve kilometres from Bukittinggi is the village of **Kota Gadang,** known for its fine silver filigree work and hand embroidery. Thirty-six kilometres from Bukittinggi on the road to Padang is **Lake Singkarak,** an ideal place for swimming, waterskiing and boating.

On the road to Padang via Lake Singkarak is the high mountain town of **Solok,** famous for its woodcarvings and traditional houses. The village of **Pandai Sikat** is 10 kilometres from Bukittinggi and has a hand-weaving industry where 1,000 looms turn out richly woven cloth. Carved wooden ornaments and furniture are also made here.

A winding road descends to **Lake Maninjau,** 36 kilometres from Bukittinggi. A crater lake, it abounds with fish and there are facilities for swimming and waterskiing. The village of **Matur** overlooking the lake gives dance performances by arrangement through local travel agents. **Payakumbuh,** a picturesque village and marketplace 35 kilometres from Bukittinggi, is known for its fine basketry. Not far away is the dramatic scenery of **Harau Canyon.**

Rimba Panti Nature Reserve is 103 kilometres from Bukittinggi. The reserve covers 3,120 hectares and the road through it is three kilometres long. There are species of monkey, bear, tiger, flying squirrel and butterfly. You can get a guide from the office at the reserve. The provincial office of the Directorate of Nature Preservation is at Padang, and can provide you with information on visiting the reserve. **Ngalau Kamang,** 15 kilometres from Bukittinggi, is a two-kilometre long cave full of stalactites and stalagmites. Torches can be hired. In **Batang Palapuh,** 12 kilometres from Bukittinggi, is the world's largest flower, the *rafflesia,* measuring up to one metre across. It blooms only in July and August. **Batusangkar** is 46 kilometres from Bukittinggi, and is the site of a former king's residence. Along the way you will see small shelters holding *prasasti,* historical stones with Hindu writing. In the town there is a fine example of a traditional Minangkabau meeting house. Five kilometres out of town are craftsmen who build replicas of the king's house, which are available for sale.

Shopping in Bukittinggi

You will find some of the same regional favourites that are also available in Padàng. The area is known for plaited mats and baskets, filigree silverwork, hand-weaving with silver and gold thread made into sarongs and headdresses, wooden carvings and coconut-shell ornaments. You can stop at the art and curio shops along Jalan Minangkabau.

Hotels in Bukittinggi

The Minang Hotel (Jl. Panorama 20A, Tel. 21120) has a beautiful view across the canyon. Dymen's International (★★★ Jl. Nawawi 1, Tel. 22781) is in a quiet area out of town with a beautiful dining room. The Benteng (★ Jl. Benteng 1, Tel. 21115) has 17 rooms near Fort de Kock. Try the **restaurants** at Dymen's or the Minang Hotel. Typical Padang food is at the Famili Restaurant, Jl. Yos. Sudarso.

Sulawesi

Less well known than Java, Bali and Sumatra is the island of Sulawesi. The orchid-shaped island, once known as the Celebes, is gaining in popularity among tourists who are attracted to its beautiful volcanoes, white beaches, marine life and distinctive cultural groups.

The island is divided into two provinces, North and South Sulawesi. The Minahasa live in North Sulawesi, where coconut plantations grow. In South Sulawesi the Torajanese live in the central mountain district and are known for their cliff burial sites and fascinating architecture. The Makassarese and Buginese in the south are known for their colourful silk and fleets of wooden sailing ships.

A popular tour of South Sulawesi is to fly to Ujung Pandang, the capital of the province, and hire a car and driver to go eight hours north

to Rantepao, the city in the heartland of Tanah Toraja with its beautiful
scenery, incredible Torajanese houses, cliffside graves and, if you are lucky
enough to be there at the right season, the festive funeral ceremonies.
While many drive directly back to Ujung Pandang after a four to five-day
tour, there are other sights if you have the time: enormous caves,
waterfalls, butterflies and beautiful beaches.

To visit North Sulawesi, fly to the provincial capital, Manado. Using
Manado as a base, see the coconut plantations, visit the hill village and
enjoy the excellent diving.

Shopping in South Sulawesi offers brilliantly coloured Buginese silk in
geometric designs accompanied by heavy gold jewellery. In Toraja there is
heavy, handloomed cotton, often with patterns of buffaloes and houses.
Baskets and woodcarving reminiscent of the woodcarvings on the fronts
of the Torajanese house are also popular.

Ujung Pandang

This city, located on the southwestern tip of Sulawesi, is the gateway to
the eastern islands of Indonesia. A thriving port with many trees and
Dutch houses, it was formerly called Makassar.

The SS *Kerinci* sails from Jakarta to Ujung Pandang weekly (see

Rice barns, Tanah Toraja

page 22). Most people arrive in Ujung Pandang at Hasanuddin Airport. Bargain on the taxi fare to town, 20 kilometres away. There are four flights daily from Jakarta and daily service to Bali, Surabaya and Manado. You may wish to begin your drive north to the Tanah Toraja area right away. You can rent a car and driver from your hotel or arrange for a **tour** of South Sulawesi through Indonesia Safari (Jl. Somba Opu 111, Tel. 21757, Telex 71172) or Pacto (Jl. Sudirman 56, Tel. 83208, Telex 71218).

Among the sights in Ujung Pandang is the **Ujung Pandang Fort,** which was built is 1545 by the tenth king of Gowa and later used by the Dutch, who named it Fort Rotterdam in 1667. Inside it you will find the **State Museum,** which is only open in the morning and has a collection of manuscripts, statues, costumes, ceramics and model sailing ships. Also in the fort complex is the **Dance and Music Conservatory,** where you may catch a practice session.

An excellent collection of **sea shells** and hundreds of species of **orchids** for show and sale are at the Bundt residence at Jalan Mochtar Lufti 15.

In the centre of the city is a small cemetery with the **grave of Prince Diponegoro,** one of Indonesia's great heroes, who was imprisoned in the fort by the Dutch for 26 years. On the outskirts of Ujung Pandang is **Paotere,** where the picturesque *pinisi* sailing boats dock. These enormous schooners are among the last fleets of sailing cargo ships in the world. A beautiful sight at sunset.

Sungguminasa, once the seat of the king of Gowa, is 11 kilometres out of Ujung Pandang. The king's residence is now a museum called Ballalompoa, where costumes and weapons are displayed.

The **tomb of Sultan Hasanuddin** (1629-1670) and those of other kings of Gowa are located off the main road nine kilometres from Ujung Pandang. Sultan Hasanuddin was famous for his bravery in fighting the Dutch colonial forces, and the airport and local university are named for him. Not far from the tomb is one of the older mosques in the area, the **Katangka Mosque** (1603).

You can make a morning **tour by boat** to Law-Lae and Samalona or Kahyangan islands about one hour away. Here you can see Bugis fishermen at work, and swim, snorkel and picnic.

Other places of interest are quite some distance from Ujung Pandang. **Bulukumba,** on the southeastern coast 153 kilometres from Ujung Pandang, has white sandy beaches and the shipyards of **Bira,** where the Bugis sailing ships are built. At **Pattae Cave,** east of Maros, about 1½ hours from Ujung Pandang, there are cave paintings between 5,000 and 10,000 years old. The largest cave in South Sulawesi is **Goa Mampu,** 34 kilometres from Watampone.

Near Watampone is the **Museum Lapawawoi,** where regalia of the kingdom of Bone is on display. **Bantimurung,** about 45 kilometres from

Ujung Pandang, is the site of beautiful waterfalls, and there are many beautiful butterflies flitting through the shrubs and over the water. Caves here have hand prints dating back 2,000 years. **Malino,** formerly the holiday resort of kings, is 74 kilometres from Ujung Pandang on the slopes of Mt Bawakaraeng, where the climate is cool and palm trees grow.

Shopping in Ujung Pandang is best along Jalan Somba Opu, where you will find brass, silver, crafts and silk. Try Art Shop at No.20, Asdor Art Shop (No.199), Mutiara (No.117A) and Paleori (No.108). To see the beautiful, colourful Buginese silks being made, visit Pertenunan Sutera Alam Sulawesi, the silk factory at Jalan Onta 408. Antique Chinese porcelain is available from Cony Karya, Jl. Pasar Ikan 26, but make sure to get an official export permit from the office at the Dutch fort.

Restaurants: For seafood try Surya Supercrab, Jl. Nusakambangan 16. Chinese food is good at the Bamboo Den, Jl. Latimojong and at Setia Restaurant, Jl. Bacan 2.

Hotels in Ujung Pandang: Raodah International (★★★ 96 rooms, Jl. Khairil Anwar 5, Tel. 7055) has a good restaurant. Grand (★★ 65 rooms, Jl. Jend. Yani 5, Tel. 5881) is in a good location. Victoria (★★ 41 rooms, Jl. Jend. Sudirman 24, Tel. 21428) is another possibility.

Tanah Toraja

The main highlight of a visit to South Sulawesi is the trip to Tanah Toraja. Although it is an eight-hour trip by rented mini-van or jeep with a driver, travellers consider it well worth it. Tanah Toraja is in the mountainous northern part of the province of South Sulawesi. The people live in fantastic houses called *tongkonan* that have enormous saddle-shaped roofs made of hundreds of pieces of bamboo that swoop to the sky. The facades are covered with geometrically carved, painted wooden panels, and some houses have buffalo horns, a sign of wealth, fixed to a long pole going up the front of the house.

Tanah Toraja is famous for its unusual burial methods. Wealthy people are buried in caves carved high up in the sides of cliffs. Covering the entrance to the graves are lifelike figures of the deceased, effigies known as *tau tau*. Ask your travel agent if you can visit a funeral ceremony, usually held at the end of the harvest season in November. These are joyous occasions, celebrations of the soul of the departed being freed into the hereafter. The funerals are held well after the actual death, sometimes even years later, in order to allow all the families and friends to save up money and make plans for these enormous, joyful occasions. There is dancing, excitement, music and colourful dress. Many buffaloes are sacrificed during the ceremonies.

As you leave Ujung Pandang for Tanah Toraja, you will drive along the coast, seeing the Buginese houses on stilts. In Pare, 150 kilometres from

Scene of a funeral ceremony, Tanah Toraja

Ujung Pandang, stop for a beer and Chinese lunch at the Sempurna
Restaurant, Jl. Bau Massepe 577.

As you come to the Tanah Toraja area you will be impressed by the
scenic beauty of the mountainous region 2,500 feet above sea level. Stay at
the town of **Rantepao,** the centre of Tanah Toraja, and make day trips
with your hired car and driver to the many interesting sights in the area.
At **Lemo,** one kilometre from Rantepao, you can see graves carved out of
solid rock with effigies lined up along the front. Best to go in the morning
when the light is right for photography. At **Londa** you can see more
hanging graves, those of the nobility. Young village guides with kerosene
lamps will take you into the caves to see skeletons and old coffins. In the
village of **Kete Kesu** wooden and bamboo carvings of Toraja design are
made. One hundred metres behind the village you can see more
Torajanese graves in cliffs. Visit **Palawa** to see Toraja village life and
typical houses. See the tombs at **Bori.** At **Pala Tokke** graves with coffins
carved from wood hang off the cliffs, and at **Sangala** is another village
with interesting graves, especially a tree grave for babies. As a break from
grave visiting, pay a visit to the village of **Tenen,** a weaving village where
the beautiful heavy cotton Torajanese cloth is made. Also visit Marante
village, where the traditional home is perched on a hill at **Siguntuk.**

Hotels in Rantepao are pleasant and comfortable. Wisma Maria II is a

good place to stay, built on the same property as a traditional rice barn and house where the owner lives. Toraja Cottages (★★★) has 63 rooms at Jl. Paku Balasara, Tel. Ujung Pandang 84146, Telex 46621 HBI IA. Misiliana (★★) has 41 rooms, Tel. 56.

North Sulawesi

The province of North Sulawesi comprises the northeastern arm of the island and stretches north into small islands much like stepping stones to the Philippines. The region has 54 mountain peaks over 25,786 square miles. There are long stretches of white sandy beach with palms and natural coral gardens. The area is one of Indonesia's richest coconut producers, and cloves and nutmeg are abundant. The people of the area, the Minahasa, are prosperous and among the most Western-minded people of Indonesia. They are gay and friendly. Because of the strong Dutch influence in the area, many speak Dutch and are Christian.

The provincial capital, **Manado,** is the chief port of North Sulawesi and home base for tourists investigating the area. There is a regular air service, often fully booked, to Ujung Pandang and Jakarta.

When visiting local villages, see the *warugas,* stone crypts with ornate carvings. **Tasik Ria,** about 20 kilometres from Manado, is a beach that is ideal for swimming, sailing, diving and fishing. **Tara-Tara** is a centre of Minahasa art, 30 kilometres south of Manado. Every Sunday at 3pm there is a two-hour performance of local dance and music. Visitors are met with the traditional *cakalele* dance and escorted to the arena where 280 people perform accompanied by the bamboo *kolintang* band. **Tondano Lake,** a two-hour drive from Manado, has ancient stone tombs in the villages of Airmadidi, Swaangan and Likupang.

Tangkoko Bauangus, near Manado's seaport of Bitung, is a nature reserve with a sandy coastline and coral gardens. The island of **Bunaken** in the Bay of Manado and the reefs around it have a wealth of coral in crystal clear waters. Marine life there is beautiful. Scuba divers can rent equipment. The best months for snorkelling and diving are from April to early September.

The **hill villages** of Tomohon, Sonder and Koombi, an hour's drive from Manado, are set in clove plantations and are known for the beauty of their houses and the lovely gardens.

Hotels in Manado: The Kawanua City Hotel (★★★) has 100 rooms on Jl. Dr Tarulangi 1, Tel. 52222. The New Queen Hotel (★) has 30 rooms, located on Jl. Wakeke 12-24, Tel. 4440.

Restaurants: The Miami, Jl. Yos Sudarso 73, serves Western and Indonesian food. Jit Hien, Jl. Panjaitan 35, is known for Chinese food. There is a good view of Manado from the mountain Pamandangan Restaurant.

Words and Phrases

Your efforts to speak Bahasa Indonesia will be greeted with pleasure and encouragement. By comparison to English and Chinese it's an easy language, so go ahead and give it a try.

Pronunciation: Individual letters only have one pronunciation, unlike English. A few minutes learning the pronunciation will help you to use the following lists of words effectively. Pronounce a as in father, c as in cheap, e as in term, g as in get, h as in hot, i as in is, j as in job, o as in also, u as in put, y as in yet, ai as in buy, ng as in singer, ngg as in finger.

And now, some handy words for you to use.

Greetings

good morning	*selamat pagi*
good afternoon	*selamat siang*
good evening	*selamat sore*
good night	*selamat malam*
goodbye (if you are going)	*selamat tinggal*
goodbye (if you are staying)	*selamat jalan*
welcome	*selamat datang*
How are you?	*Apa kabar?*
fine	*kabar baik*
excuse me; I'm sorry	*ma'af*
please (offering)	*silahkan*
please (asking for help)	*tolong*

Forms of Address

Sir; Mr	*Pak*
Mrs; Madame	*Ibu*

Personal Pronouns

I	*saya*
you	*saudara* or *anda*
he; she	*dia*
we	*kami* or *kita*
you	*saudara*
they	*mereka*

Numbers

one	*satu*
two	*dua*
three	*tiga*

four	empat
five	lima
six	enam
seven	tuju
eight	delapan
nine	sembilan
ten	sepuluh
eleven	sebelas
twelve	duabelas
thirteen	tigabelas
twenty	duapuluh
thirty	tiga puluh
31	tiga puluh satu
32	tiga puluh dua
100	seratus
200	dua ratus
250	dua ratus lima puluh
1,000	seribu
2,000	dua ribu
10,000	sepuluh ribu
20,000	dua puluh ribu

Time

century	abad
year	tahun
month	bulan
week	minggu
day	hari
hour	jam
minute	menit
Monday	Senin
Tuesday	Selasa
Wednesday	Rabu
Thursday	Kamis
Friday	Jum'at
Saturday	Sabtu
Sunday	Minggu
What time is it?	Jam berapa?
nine o'clock	jam sembilan
tomorrow	besok
yesterday	kemarin
how long?	berapa lama?

Questions

What is that?	*Apa itu?*
Who are you?	*Siapa anda?*
what?	*apa?*
how?	*bagaimana?*
how many; how much?	*berapa?*
where?	*dimana?*
when?	*kapan?*
why?	*mengapa?*

Travel Words

bank	*bank*
map	*peta*
telephone	*telepon*
car	*mobil*
taxi	*taksi*
pedicab	*becak*
bus	*bis*
luggage	*barang*
aeroplane	*kapal terbang*
ship	*kapal laut*
hotel	*hotel*
post office	*kantor pos*
train	*kareta api*
airport	*lapangan terbang*
petrol station	*pom bensin*
city	*kota*
I want to go to...	*Saya mau pergi ke...*
What is the fare?	*Berapa ongkos?*
stop!	*berhenti!*
driver	*sopir*
ticket	*karcis*
slow down!	*pelan pelan!*

Shopping

store	*toko*
market	*pasar*
I want to buy	*Saya mau beli*
how much	*berapa*
too expensive	*terlalu mahal*
OK	*baiklah*
cheap	*murah*
money	*uang*

cigarettes	*rokok*
matches	*korek api*
rupiah	*rupiah*
Rps 10,000	*sepuluh ribu rupiah*
crafts	*kerajinan*
stamp	*perangko*
dictionary	*kamus*
newspaper	*surat kabar*
ceramics	*keramik*
batik	*batik*

Directions

left	*kiri*
right	*kanan*
far	*jauh*
near	*dekat*
straight ahead	*terus*

Sightseeing

mosque	*mesjid*
church	*gereja*
museum	*musium*
street	*jalan*
information office	*kantor penerangan*
traditional houses	*rumah adat*
zoo	*kebun binatang*
port	*pelabuhan*
dance performance	*pertunjukan tari-tarian*
palace	*istana* or *kraton*
room	*kamar*
bed	*tempat tidur*
toilet	*kamar kecil*
bathroom	*kamar mandi*
swimming pool	*kolam renang*
electricity	*listrik*
restaurant	*restoran; rumah makan*
eat	*makan*
drink	*minum*
plate	*piring*
glass	*gelas*
cup	*cangkir*
knife	*pisau*
fork	*garpu*

| spoon | sendok |
| without ice | tanpa es |

Food and Drink

tea	teh
coffee	kopi
egg	telor
bread	roti
butter	mentega
cheese	keju
Coca-Cola	Koka-Kola
sugar	gula
milk	susu
rice	nasi
fried rice	nasi goreng
fried noodles	mie goreng
skewered meat	sate
chicken	ayam
beef	daging sapi
pork	daging babi
prawns	udang
fish	ikan
banana	pisang
papaya	papaya
mango	mangga
pineapple	nanas
hot	panas
spicy	pedas
cold	dingin
rice porridge	bubur
vegetable	sayur
fruit	buah

Health

I need a doctor	Saya memerlukan dokter
I am sick	Saya sakit
very sick	sakit keras
dentist	dokter gigi
drugstore	apotik
medicine	obat
hospital	rumah sakit

Other Useful Words

insecticide	*obat nyamuk*
I don't understand	*Saya tidak mengerti*
yes	*ya*
good	*baiklah*
no	*tidak*
you may not	*tidak boleh*
you may	*boleh*
forbidden	*dilarang*
broken	*rusak*
open	*buka*
closed	*tutup*
entrance	*masuk*
exit	*keluar*
child	*anak*
children	*anak anak* or *anak²* (plurals are created by repeating the noun or by placing a 2 after it)
look out!	*awas*
be careful!	*hati hati*

And a final note: *Semoga saudara saudara sangat terhibur sewakatu di Indonesia.* This means 'I hope you have a wonderful time in Indonesia'. *Selamat jalan!* Have a good trip!

Index

A

Abdullah, Basuki 41
Aceh 112
Affandi 71
Agastya 68, 87
airlines 19, 37
airports 19
Al-Azhar Mosque 44
Ambarita 120
Ambon 19, 21
amusement parks 48
Ancol 48
animism 10, 11, 112
antiques 45, 57, 76, 81, 85, 102, 116
aquarium 80
arts and crafts 27-28, 44-47, 48, 60, 69, 71, 81, 101, 105-109, 125, 129
aviary 44

B

backgammon 100
Bahasa Indonesia 8, 10, 133-140
Bali 87-111
Baliem Valley 12, 21
Bandung 21, 28, 56, 57-60
Bangli 89, 101
banking 25
Banten 16
Bantimurung 128-129
Banuwangi 80
bargaining 27
Barong dance 101, 105, 108
bars 50
baskets 26, 28, 45, 85, 107, 108, 124, 125, 126
Batak 9, 53, 112, 113, 117, 118, 120, 121
Batam 19
Batang Palapuh 125
Batavia 16, 36
Bat Cave temple 103
Bateson, Gregory 89
bathrooms 26
batik 7, 15, 18, 28, 45, 61, 64, 65, 67, 71, 72, 77, 81, 107, 116
Batu 80, 85

Batubulan 105, 108
Batusangkar 125
Bay of Bungus 123
becak 20, 57, 65, 76, 114
Bedugul 110
Belawan 114
Belo, Jane 89
bemo 20, 96, 101, 120
Bengkulu 113
Besakih 14, 100, 102
Biak 19
Bima train 19, 79
Bira 128
Bogor 48, 56-57, 62
Bona 105, 108
Bonnet, Rudolf 89
books 32, 56, 110
Bori 130
Borneo 9
Borobudur 10, 13, 29, 64, 65, 67-68
botanical gardens 56, 117
bowling 47, 110, 116
Brastagi 16, 113, 117
British East India Company 16
Buddhism 9, 13, 14, 67-68
Bukit Lawang 113, 115
Bukittinggi 21, 112, 113, 122, 124-125
bull races 80, 83-84
Bulukumba 128
Bunaken 132
buses 19, 21, 37, 100-101, 113

C

cakalele dance 132
Campuan 97, 99, 104, 108
candi (temples) 13, 68, 77, 80, 85-87
canting 15
cap 28, 71
Carita Beach 56, 63-64
cars 19, 20, 80, 101, 125, 128
Celuk 108
Central Java 64-77
ceramics 28, 43, 45, 60, 109, 128
children 25
Chinatown 40, 41
Christianity 9, 10, 112, 132
cinema 49, 52
Cirebon 56, 60-61

cliff graves 129, 130
climate 18
clothing 18, 91, 107
colonialism 16, 57, 89
credit cards 25
cremations 14, 97, 103
cruises 21-22
currency 19, 25
Customs regulations 19

D
deHoutman, Cornelius 89
delman 20, 101
Denpasar 101, 108, 109, 111
dinner shows 49, 92, 99, 100
discos 29, 49, 51, 92, 100
diving 28, 48, 56, 61-62, 109, 126, 132
doctors 24, 25, 92, 111
dokar 20
drinks 25, 30
driving 19, 57, 101
Durga 68
Dutch 15-16
Dutch East India Company 16, 41

E
East Java 77-87
electricity 18
embassies 36-37
entertainment 29, 49-50, 81
etiquette 31
exchange rate 25
exit/re-entry permit 19

F
family planning 7
Fatahillah 36
festivals and holidays 29, 104
fire dance 105
fiscal tax 19
flea market 44, 45
flora and fauna 29-30, 56
Flores 9, 21
food 25, 30, 53-56, 97-100
foreign missions 36-37, 83
Fort de Kock 124, 125
Fort Speelwijk 16
fruits 30

G
Galungan 29, 104
gamelan 14
Gampingan 71
Gang Bengkok Mosque 115
geography 9
Gereja Emmanuel 43
Gereja Sion 41
Gilimanuk 80
Glodok 40, 41
Goa Gajah Elephant Cave 99
Goa Mampu 128
go-karts 48
golf 28, 48, 92, 110, 115, 117, 120
gong factory 56
government 16-17
Gundaling Hill 117

H
hairdressers 47
haji 9
handicrafts 27, 43, 45, 69, 105-109, 125, 129
Harau Canyon 124
health 24
Hendra 41
Hinduism 9, 10, 13, 14, 68, 88
hiking 28, 57, 113, 117
history 10, 36, 64, 77, 87, 112-113
holidays 29, 104
homestays 96, 97
horseback riding 28, 29, 57, 80, 84, 85, 110, 117, 118
hospitals 24, 60
hotels:
    Bali 89-97
    Bandung 60
    Batu 85
    Brastagi 117
    Bukittinggi 125
    Carita 63
    Cirebon 61
    Jakarta 50-53
    Lake Toba 120-121
    Madura 83
    Malang 85
    Manado 132
    Medan 116

Mount Bromo 84
Padang 123
Puncak 57
Samudra 62
Selecta 85
Surabaya 81-82
Tanah Toraja 130-132
Thousand Islands 61-62
Tretes 84
Ujung Pandang 129
Yogyakarta 73
Hudoyo, Sapto 71

I
Ibu Tien 17
ikat 12, 28, 103
immigration 18
Imogiri 69
Irian Jaya 9, 21
Islam 9, 10, 14, 56, 60, 88, 112-113
Istana Merdeka 43
Istana Negara 43
Istana Sultan Deli 114
Istiqlal Mosque 43

J
Jago temple 87
Jakarta 33-56
Jakarta Pusat 41-44
Japanese occupation 16
Jati 107
Java 33-87
Java Man 10, 43, 64, 77
Jawi temple 80, 87
Jayakarta 36
jazz 50, 51
jewellery 7, 46, 69, 76, 77, 108, 116, 126
jogging 47, 110

K
Kabanjahe 117, 118
kain prada 28
Kalimantan 9, 21
Kamasan 108
Kartika 71
Kasongan 69
Katangka Mosque 128
kecak dance 105

Kediri kingdom 77, 88
Keluarga Berencana 7
Kerapan Besar 83-84
Kete Kesu 130
Kidal temple 80, 87
Kintamani 99, 101
klenteng (temple) 10, 41
Klungkung 100, 102, 103, 108
Kota 36, 40, 45
Kota Gadang 124
Kota Gede 69
Krakatau 63
kraton 14, 15, 61, 65, 72, 76, 84
kris 45, 65, 67, 76, 105, 108
Kuningan 29, 104
Kunst, Jaap 89
Kusudiarjo, Bagong 72
Kusumba 103
Kuta Beach 25, 87, 91, 93-96, 99, 102, 109, 110

L
Lake Maninjau 124
Lake Singkarak 124
Lake Toba 21, 112, 113, 114, 116-121
language 8, 133-140
leather 28, 45, 71
Lebaran 8, 29
lectures 49
Legian Beach 91, 96, 109
legong dance 100, 105
Lemo 130
Lingga 118
Londa 130
Lombok 21, 88
lurik 77

M
Madura 80, 83-84
Mahabharata 77, 87, 88
Mahakam River 21
Majapahit Dynasty 13, 65, 79, 85, 87
Makassar 126
Malacca 112
Malang 80, 85-87
Malik, Adam 40
Malino 129
Maluku 15

Manado 19, 21, 126, 132
mandi 26
maps 116
Marante 130
markets 44, 46, 72, 76, 77, 85, 123
Maros 128
Mas 107, 108
masks 69, 76, 108
Mataram empire 69, 79
Matur 124
Mayeur, Le 104
McPhee, Colin 89
Mead, Margaret 89
Mecca 9
Medan 19, 113, 114-116
media 24
medical facilities 24
Mendut temple 10, 29, 68
Mengwi, 89, 100, 102
Menteng 36, 45
Mesjid Raya 114
Minahasa 125, 132
Minang food 85
Minangkabau 112, 121, 124, 125
Moluccas 9
money 25
monkeys 102
mosques 9, 33, 43, 44, 60, 61, 114, 115,
    128
motorcycles 101
Mount Agung 102
Mount Batur 101
Mount Bromo 80, 84-85
Mount Lawu 76, 77
Mount Merapi 65, 76, 124
Mount Sibayak 117
Mount Sinabung 117
museums 40-41, 43, 44, 56, 65-67, 76, 77,
    84, 104, 117, 123, 124, 128
musholla 9
music cassettes 46, 56, 91
Muslim 9, 14, 15, 29, 33, 83, 112-113, 121

N
national development 16-17
National Monument 41
National Museum 10, 11, 12, 13, 16, 36,
    43

nature reserves 29-30, 63-64, 115-116,
    124-125, 132
Negrito 8
newspapers 24
Ngadisari 84
Ngalau Kamang 125
Ngarai Sianok 124
Nias 21, 112, 113
nightspots 29, 49-50, 100
Nusa Dua 89, 93, 109
Nyuhkuning 104

O
oceanarium 48
odalan (temple festival) 103-104
office hours 23
oil 17
Orang-utan Rehabilitation Centre 113,
    115
orchids 44, 56, 128

P
Pabatu 117
Padang 21, 22, 113, 115, 122-123, 124, 125
Padang food 7, 53, 116, 122, 125
Padris 113
Pala Tokke 130
Palawa 130
Palembang 112
Pamekasan 83, 84
Panataran temple 80, 87
Pancasila 17
Pandaan 80, 81
Pandai Sikat 124
Panguruan 120
Paotere 128
Pare 129-130
Pasar Ikan 40, 41
pasars (markets) 26, 28, 46, 72, 76, 77,
    85, 123
Pattae Cave 128
Pawon temple 68
Payakumbuh 124
pedicabs (becak) 20, 57, 65, 76, 114
Pejeng 88
Peliatan 23, 97
Pemantang Siantur 117
Pematung Purba 118

Penang 21, 113, 114
Penataran Sasih temple 88
Pengosekan 108
performing arts 49, 56, 60, 72-73, 81,
   104-105, 123, 132
Pertamina 17
Petroleum Club 43
photography 30, 41
Phuket 21
pici 9
pizza 49, 99
plants 30, 117
Polo, Marco 112
population 8
Portuguese 15, 41, 89, 112
postal services 24
Prajnaparamita 43
Prambanan temple 13, 64, 65, 68-69, 72,
   76
Prapat 113, 117, 118, 120, 121
prasasti 125
Puasa (fasting month) 29
Pulau Putri 21, 61
Puncak 56, 57, 62

R
radio 24
Raffles, Sir Stamford 16
rafflesia 125
raksasas 87, 108
Ramadan 29, 53
Ramayana 68, 69, 72, 87, 88, 105
Rantepao 126, 130
Raya 117
reading 32
religion 9
restaurants 30, 53-56, 57, 60, 61, 62, 73,
   81, 85, 97-100, 116, 129, 130, 132
Rimba Panti Nature Reserve 124-125
roadside stalls 45

S
Sadali 41
Sailendra dynasty 67
sailing 28, 92, 109, 110, 132
Saleh, Raden 41, 65
Samosir island 113, 117, 120
Samudra Beach 21, 56, 62

Sangala 130
Sangeh 102
Sangiran 77
Sanur Beach 87, 89-93, 99, 109, 110
Sarinah's Department Store 16, 27, 43,
   45, 46
sate 7, 25, 51, 53, 99, 100
scuba diving 61, 62, 132
sea shells 41, 56, 61, 128
Selecta 80, 85
Semarang 10, 21
Senayan Sports Stadium 16
shipping 21-22, 113, 126
shopping 26-28
Sibolangit 117
Sibolga 21
Siguntuk 130
silat 123
silver 7, 27, 45, 46, 69, 101, 108, 124, 125,
   129
Simanindo 120
Singasari dynasty 79, 85, 87
Singasari temple 87
Si Piso Piso Waterfall 118
Slipi 44
snorkelling 7, 29, 56, 61-62, 109, 128, 132
Solo (Surakarta) 73-77
Solok 124
songket 28
Spice Islands 15
Spies, Walter 89, 97
sports 28, 47-48, 51, 109-110
squash 47, 51, 110, 116
Srivijaya 13, 112
stone carving 67, 68, 77, 87, 103, 108,
   117, 132
Sudjoyono 41
Suharto 16, 36
Sukapura 84
Sukarno 16, 17
Sukawati 108
Sulawesi 125-132
Sultan Agung 69
Sultan Hasanuddin 128
Sumatra 111-125
Sumba 12
Sumbawa 88
Sumenep 84

Sunda 56
Sunda Kelapa 36
Sungguminasa 128
Surabaya 79-83
Surakarta (Solo) 73-77
surfing 109
sushi 53

T
Taman Ayun 102
Taman Fatahillah 40
Tamanjaya 64
Taman Mini Indonesia 33, 44
Tamon Sari 67
Tampaksiring 99, 101
Tanah Lot 102
Tanah Toraja 21, 126, 128, 129-132
Tangkoko Bauangus 132
Tanjung Perak 80
Tao island 120
Tara-Tara 132
Taruma Negara 36
Tasik Ria 132
tau tau (effigy) 129
Tawangmangu 77
taxis 20, 37, 65, 76, 96, 114
Tebbing Tinggi 117
telegram 24
telephone 24
television 24
telex 24
Teluk Bayur 122
temples 9-10, 13, 67-69, 76, 77, 80, 81, 85-87, 103-104
Tenen 130
Tenganan 102
Tenggarese guides 84
tennis 47, 51, 57, 62, 87, 93, 110, 116, 120
terracotta 69, 72, 92, 109
textiles 17, 28, 44, 45, 46, 60, 67, 77, 101, 108, 112, 116, 121, 123, 124, 126, 130
Thousand Islands 7, 48, 56, 61-62
Timor 9
tipping 25
toilets 26
Tomok 120, 121
Tondano Lake 132
Tongging 118

topeng 108
tourist information offices 29, 83, 85, 104, 123
tours 20-21, 37, 80, 84-85, 100-103, 113, 117, 124, 128
trade 17
trains 19
trance dance 81, 105
transportation 19
travel agencies 19, 21, 37, 57, 80, 100-101, 113, 124, 128
Tretes 84
Trusmi 61
Tuk Tuk 120
tulis 28, 71
Turtle Island 109

U
Ubud 23, 91-92, 96-97, 99, 104, 108, 109
Ujung Kulon 63-64
Ujung Pandang 16, 22, 125, 126-129
ulos (textile gift) 121

V
vaccinations 24
visas 18-19
volcanoes 9, 29, 60, 63, 64, 65, 76, 77, 84, 101, 111, 124, 125

W
Waisak 10, 29
warugas 132
waterfalls 84, 117, 118, 126, 129
waterskiing 61, 92, 109, 118, 120, 124
wayang 28, 41
West Java 56-64
West Sumatra 121-125
wildlife 29-30, 63, 124-125
windsurfing 87, 92, 109
woodcarving 27-28
words and phrases 133-138
World Wildlife Fund 30

Y
Yogyakarta 65-73

Z
zoos 48, 56, 80, 115, 124